The Summer House Cookbook

The Summer House Cookbook

Easy Recipes for When You Have Better Things to Do With Your Time

Debra Ponzek and Geralyn Delaney Graham

CLARKSON POTTER/PUBLISHERS

NEW YORK

7/2003 Sen Fund 30,—

Published by Clarkson Potter/Publishers, New York, New York
Member of the Crown Publishing Group, a division of Random House, Inc.
www.randomhouse.com

CLARKSON N. POTTER is a trademark and POTTER and colophon are registered
trademarks of Random House, Inc.

Printed in China

Design by Maggie Hinders

Library of Congress Cataloging-in-Publication Data
The summer house cookbook: easy recipes for when you have better things to do with
your time / Debra Ponzek and Geralyn Delaney Graham.—1st ed.
   1. Cookery. 2. Entertaining. I. Ponzek, Debra. II. Graham, Geralyn Delaney.
TX714 .S8475 2003
641.5—dc21   2002038136

ISBN 0-609-60822-3

10 9 8 7 6 5 4 3 2 1

First Edition

to my angelic children, Remy, Cole, and Gray,
whose smiles and laughter make my heart soar every day.
And to my husband, Greg, who has always supported
my career and choices without restraint.

D P

to my mom, my first food mentor, who nurtured
my passion for cooking through the three delicious
meals she lovingly prepared our family every day.
To my dad, who truly knew how to enjoy each minute
of summer vacation at the beach with his family.
And to my husband, Patrick, whose endless support
(and endless cups of coffee brought to me in bed
on Saturday mornings) through the writing of
my first book can never be measured.

G D G

Contents

preface

Debra and I met in the autumn of 1989, when we both worked at Montrachet, Drew Nieporent's critically acclaimed French restaurant that pioneered the now-popular neighborhood of Tribeca. Debra was the executive chef, a young woman in her late twenties who had already earned a three-star review from the *New York Times*—a feat she would accomplish two more times during her seven-year tenure there. She was one of the top young Americans cooking in New York City, and one of the only women. She had already won the coveted Rising Star Chef award from the James Beard Foundation, and a very exclusive French culinary group awarded her an honor never before given to an American.

I, on the other hand, was passionate about food but not quite yet up to the three-star mark. Having waitressed during college, after graduation I pursued a very corporate career in public relations. But, in my late twenties, bored and lacking fun in my life, I turned to my avocation, food. By some miracle of fate, Drew hired me to work at Montrachet as the day manager, where I did everything from taking reservations to planning private parties and waiting tables. There, Debra and I became fast friends.

We had always talked about writing a book together, but life—including developing careers, husbands, and children—kept getting in our way. Finally, in 1999, ten years after we became friends, we hunkered down to write a proposal. We wanted to do something more simple and casual than a restaurant book, something more in keeping with the way we liked to cook and entertain at home. We looked to shared experiences and talked about the way we ate growing up.

Both of our families spent summers on the shore—Debra's vacationed on Cape Cod each year and my family lived five minutes from the New Jersey shore—and so many of our best food memories seemed to revolve around summer. We both loved shopping with our moms for fruits and vegetables at the fabulous farms that can be found throughout the Northeast; we learned how to finesse a grill by watching our dads cook our summer dinners, and oh, the lobster feasts!

They weren't the fanciest meals we ate all year, but they were definitely some of the best. We started to talk about how our families had created such memorable occasions with such minimalist preparations and cooking equipment, and we recognized it could in large part be attributed to what we came to call the "summer house state of mind," an easygoing attitude and casual approach that made every meal taste better and every party feel like fun. It's an attitude we think is worth cultivating all year long, and it gave us the guiding principle for this, our first collaboration.

Debra and I tested and wrote all of the recipes at her home in Greenwich, Connecticut, using no special equipment (Debra still hasn't forgiven me for making her test every recipe that called for a food processor in her blender), eschewing restaurant-like stocks and fancy ingredients. We delved into our childhoods for favorite summer recipes and looked to our many adventures eating and traveling together and with our families for recipe ideas. And most important, we discussed how we enjoyed cooking and entertaining during the warmer months now that we both live outside Manhattan and juggle husbands, kids, dogs and cats, not to mention hectic careers.

So, enjoy the summer! Go to the beach, swim at the lake, play a few sets of tennis or a round of golf, take a hike in the woods, ride your bike, or relish an entire day of reading in a hammock. If you have a deep culinary spirit, visit local farm stands, fish stores, and lobster pounds, and forage for the best raw ingredients that this wonderful season offers. Then come home, open this book, and relish cooking and eating an awesome meal.

—Geralyn Delaney Graham

Introduction:
The Summer House
State of Mind

There are different rules for cooking in the summer, and there is a different state of mind entirely about eating. Some people who love to cook during the rest of the year turn off their stoves as soon as Memorial Day arrives, focus on outdoor activities, and plan their next meal around the closest restaurant or takeout shop. Others we know wait all year for their weekend share in the country or a week or two at their summer house on the lake or in the mountains; there, free of responsibilities and a time-crunched schedule, they take daily pleasure from the relaxing ritual of cooking. Most of us are somewhere in the middle.

No matter which camp you belong to, one thing is certain—summer appetites crave simplicity. Ripe fruits and vegetables picked fresh from the vine and eaten raw or drizzled with a little something, simply prepared fish, cooling salads, anything off the grill, and tall, refreshing drinks—during the summer, less really *is* more.

But as anyone who has rented a vacation house or had a share at the beach—or even has a year-round weekend retreat—knows, some advance preparation can save you precious playtime later and offers you a better chance for good eating. We remember our first tenuous attempts at cooking away from home—there are some hilarious stories and a few sad little meals that resulted—before we adjusted our strategies. We have been known to plan all of our meals for a weekend in the Hamptons ahead of time and take all the ingredients with us on the jitney from Manhattan. We've sent a box of favorite foods on the plane with our clothes when we vacationed in the Caribbean. And for one girls-only weekend, a friend of Geralyn's flew in her favorite burritos and enchiladas from her hometown in California and all we had to do when we arrived at our house Friday night was squeeze a couple dozen limes for pitcherfuls of margaritas and heat up the food. Still, when the mercury climbs and the dress code is baseball caps and flip-flops, a more spontaneous mode of cooking seems to fit the bill. And it's easy if you've set the stage properly.

The most difficult part about cooking away from the comforts of your home kitchen is deciding what equipment and seasonings to bring. It's a bit like packing shoes: Sure, you want to bring those strappy pink sandals that perfectly match your sexy slip dress and the great pair of espadrilles that you bought last summer on sale, but do you really want to drag them along to wear just once? Same thing with your pasta roller, your special baking equipment, and all those herbs and spices you rely on in your pantry that you might be tempted to schlepp just in case you need them.

It would be great to surprise your friends with fresh tortellini, but wouldn't they be just as happy with a refreshing orzo salad with a ginger oil you cleverly brought from home—and wouldn't your vacation memories be a bit more exciting without the extra time in the kitchen?

As soon as you rent your house, call ahead and get the lowdown on your kitchen, so that you know exactly what to expect. But don't worry if your gadget drawer only has a swivel-blade peeler, a whisk, and an old-fashioned box grater; you can still make 95 percent of the recipes that follow. For those of you lucky enough to have a well-equipped kitchen in your year-round country house or who plan to enjoy summer right at home on your deck or by your pool, you don't need to be concerned about these details. Still, hauling out the food processor, the mandoline, or the standing mixer isn't exactly the way we want to spend a sunny afternoon, but if your kitchen has them and that's your idea of relaxing (and yes, of course we can relate to that), go ahead.

The other part of planning that's essential to the summer house state of mind has to do with saving time. Call it multitasking for summer minimalism: If you're turning on the oven to roast a yummy chicken for dinner, why not roast two and have enough to make either of our delicious chicken salad recipes? When you're doing your cleanup from tonight's dinner, take five minutes to marinate a piece of meat or fish for the next night's grilling adventure. At the farm stand, buy enough fruit not just to eat for snacks, but to bake a pie, or blend into a breakfast shake, or transform into a quick and elegant cold fruit soup.

Now a word about leftovers. As you can probably tell, we enjoy thinking about and planning our next meal. But when it's a choice between cooking a new meal and eating leftovers and having more hours of leisure in the sun, we'll take the latter option every time. So leftovers are our secret weapon.

It seems to us that leftovers get a bad rap simply because they're often not given the creative attention they deserve. Using leftovers is just like accessorizing; that little black dress can be dressed up or down and take on an amazing array of looks with the right shoes or jewelry. Same for leftovers. Cold sliced leg of lamb on two pieces of bread with mustard doesn't sound so appetizing, but stuff it into a pita pocket with Moroccan eggplant, oven-roasted tomatoes, and a dollop of black olive tapenade, and you've got a great sandwich going.

We invite you to embrace the possibility of leftovers; we have sprinkled our leftover suggestions throughout, including ideas for terrific sandwich possibilities. Think about roasting a whole pork loin or cooking an additional lobster to ensure you'll have extra. Try making some of the spreads and accompaniments that go with each dish. In a day or two, your refrigerator and pantry will hold all the elements for some really great meals that require nothing more than opening up a few containers.

No matter where your summer house is—by the shore, off a bucolic backcountry road, or on the roof of your apartment building—summer offers a great array of simple, straightforward, and perfectly ripe ingredients for you to enjoy. A local farm stand provides the makings for flavorful, easy-to-prepare side dishes, the base for wonderful main-course salads, and the raw ingredients for a light fruit dessert. If your retreat is on the coast, you have access to pristine fish and seafood pulled out of the water just hours before you eat them. And take advantage of the local shopping; a trip to the bakery can add some dense, crusty bread to pack with fruit and cheese for an impromptu picnic, and a homey purchased dessert will give you more playtime during the day and less prep time at dinner.

Let's face it, it's summer, it's vacation. So do your initial planning, but then relax and slip into that summer state of mind—what more do you really need for a great dinner besides some good wine and good friends?

The
Summer
House
Pantry

Don't be surprised to find that when vacation rolls around and you wake up in your summer house all ready to cook, a funny thing happens. That Moroccan tajine with preserved lemons that looked like a fun project back home just sounds fussy after a relaxing day outdoors. Recipes calling for all kinds of exotic seasonings are great for other times, but vacation and summer call for a pared-down larder to fit your simpler approach to cooking, shopping, and entertaining.　We've found that a very strategically stocked pantry of staples and some make-to-take items you mix up at home—probably no more than you can pack into your 10 gallon lobster pot—plus a quick stop at the fishmonger, farm stand, or country store, can yield a nearly endless menu of irresistible summer food. So you'll never find yourself buying new jars of seasonings you already have at home for the single teaspoon you need for a recipe. See our list of rock-bottom essentials on page 20.

GETTING READY TO GO

There's nothing more frustrating than going into a strange kitchen with dreams of beautiful dinners just waiting to be prepared to find that the owner has given you the basic college dorm setup. So, when you call ahead to find out how the kitchen is stocked, don't be afraid to ask exactly what is there. If you have your heart set on a lobster feast, is there a pot big enough to cook lobsters? Does the gadget drawer include the basics like a bottle opener, a can opener, and a corkscrew? Sure, you can get all of these things at the local market, but they are just as easy to pack in your car or in your box of dry goods and equipment. We have only three "must haves" on our summer house equipment list, and if the house isn't equipped with them, it really is important to take them with you:

- good, sharp knives
- a blender to make everything from refreshing drinks to protein-packed breakfast shakes and healthful vegetable soups
- a grill and good grilling tongs; the grill doesn't have to be a fancy brand—even a small hibachi will do—but a grill is essential to summer house cooking

Only two kinds of oil—canola and a good extra-virgin olive—are used in all of the recipes. And while we are usually willing to try substituting things here and there, we don't advise substituting for these oils. Both are readily available in even small grocery stores these days, all of the recipes have been tested using these two oils, and we really believe they make a huge difference in the resulting flavor. While a few different vinegars are used throughout, you can get away with as few as one strong one such as red wine or champagne to add a clean, acidic balance to vinaigrettes and sauces, and one sweet one such as balsamic or sherry to enhance the flavor of sun-ripened fruits and vegetables.

We have included a section that contains make-ahead specialty items as well as recipes that are staple ingredients for other dishes in the book (see pages 19 to 33). Think herb-flavored oils that can be made at home and taken with you to drizzle over steamed vegetables and blended into vinaigrettes. Or marinades and dry rubs that can be made in five minutes the night before to season a piece of fish or meat so that tomorrow's dinner just needs a quick grilling or sauté. Specialty items such as a crème fraîche for a dip or dessert are included in case the local market doesn't carry them. All of these can be made ahead and taken with you to enhance the culinary side of your vacation—and make you feel and look smart when you entertain, and reduce trips to the market.

If you are like us, you'll want to get that one "big shop" at the grocery for staples and things you need all week long out of the way as soon as you arrive. Then the rest of the shopping can be part of the vacation experience—swinging by the local fish store on the way home from the beach (or even catching your own dinner), or turning an early-morning stop at the farm stand for fresh herbs, fruits, and veggies into an adventure.

We've included a suggested pantry of items to take with you or to buy on arrival; you don't necessarily need everything, but it does include all of the staples you'll need to cook everything in the book. If your palate runs toward Middle Eastern or Asian, make sure your pantry is stocked with cumin, soy sauce, and wasabi; if you love the flavors of the Mediterranean, make some of the herb-flavored oils that follow, and stock up on garlic, lemons, and anchovies; and if you are an avid baker, shop for those specialty items when you go for that run to the grocery store, including disposable pans so that you don't have to worry about taking your great aunt Lucy's favorite Bundt pan with you.

Make-to-Take Staples for the Summer House Pantry

The recipes that follow are staple items that are building blocks to other recipes in the book. Here you'll find the key to making your own mayo and crème fraîche, and in keeping with our summer house philosophy, we urge you to try these if you have the inclination and the passion—otherwise, you can purchase good-quality versions in your local market. We do want to tempt you to try some of the flavored oils, marinades, and vinaigrettes, though; they are really easy to make and we guarantee you that the small amount of effort involved can turn a plain pasta salad or cole slaw into something quite heavenly. And, if we may say so, we have yet to find a bottled equivalent that can complete with them!

Roasted Garlic

MAKES 2 HEADS

Roasted garlic keeps well in the refrigerator, so double or triple this recipe. It's an effortless way to add flavor to salads, dressings, or dips. Spread it on toasted slices of day-old baguette to make instant garlic bread for dinner.

2 whole heads of garlic

2 tablespoons extra-virgin olive oil

Preheat the oven to 400°F.

Cut off the top third of the garlic heads crosswise to expose the cloves. Drizzle each head with a tablespoon of the oil and wrap in aluminum foil. Place the garlic on a baking sheet and roast in the oven for about 40 minutes, or until soft. Allow to cool, then squeeze the garlic cloves out of their skins.

Store the garlic in plastic wrap or covered with olive oil in a glass jar up to 2 weeks in the refrigerator.

Pantry List

DRY PANTRY ITEMS

Sea salt

Black peppercorns and a pepper mill

Canola oil

Extra-virgin olive oil

Vinegar (pick at least two; they are listed in the order of how many recipes they are used in): balsamic, red wine, champagne, sherry

Dijon mustard

Herbes de Provence

Garlic

Cumin

Cayenne

Granulated sugar

Honey

Low-sodium chicken or vegetable broth

Kitchen twine or heavy string

Nonstick cooking spray

REFRIGERATOR ITEMS

Eggs (organic if possible)

Unsalted butter

Lemons, limes, oranges

Shallots

Fresh rosemary and thyme

Fresh cilantro

Fresh ginger

Basil

Jalapeño pepper

SPECIALTY ITEMS

(used in 3 recipes or less)

Anchovy fillets

Wasabi powder

Soy sauce

Sesame seeds

Sesame oil

Rice wine vinegar

Canned chipotle peppers

Curry powder

Coriander seed

Fresh Mayonnaise

MAKES 1 CUP

While we are big fans of good-quality prepared mayonnaise like Hellmann's, there is nothing like the fresh, delicate flavor of homemade. You'll become a true believer once you taste the difference it makes in a seafood recipe like the East Hampton Crab Salad (page 62), and it can be whipped up in less than 5 minutes in a blender. It does contain raw eggs, so choose very fresh ones from a reliable—preferably organic—source.

2 large egg yolks

¾ cup extra-virgin olive oil

1 to 2 tablespoons water

Juice of ½ lemon, or to taste

Sea salt and freshly ground black pepper

In a blender or food processor, whip the yolks until pale, about 1 minute. With the motor running, slowly drizzle in the olive oil in a very slow stream, until the mayonnaise begins to emulsify. As it thickens, add a few drops of water to loosen the texture, up to 2 tablespoons if necessary. Add lemon juice to taste and season with salt and pepper.

Transfer the mayonnaise to a glass or plastic container with a tight lid. The mayonnaise can be stored in the refrigerator for up to 2 weeks.

Crème Fraîche

MAKES 3 CUPS

Crème fraîche is one of those staple ingredients we reach for without a thought when we're home, but can rarely find outside specialty stores when we're visiting our favorite summer vacation spots. Fortunately, it's easy to make and keeps well, so we always have a batch on hand. Keep in mind that crème fraîche needs to be made at least 2½ days before using. In a pinch, you can substitute sour cream.

3 cups heavy cream

2 tablespoons buttermilk

In a large bowl, stir the cream and buttermilk together. Cover the bowl tightly with plastic wrap. Let the mixture stand at room temperature for 36 hours, or until it has thickened. Then refrigerate for at least 24 hours and up to 10 days before using. The crème fraîche will continue to thicken in the refrigerator.

INFUSED OILS AND SPICE BLENDS

Infused oils are a simple trick to add a subtle depth of flavor to the quickly cooked dishes we all enjoy during the warmer months. We use these oils in a variety of recipes, and once you have got them in your pantry, you'll find even more ways to enjoy them, from drizzling on bread and fresh veggies to substituting them for plain extra-virgin olive oil in a favorite vinaigrette recipe.

Dry spice blends are a quick and easy way to add flavor to fish, chicken, meat, and vegetables, especially when cooking on the grill. We limited the number of ingredients we used, and focused on getting the right combination to bring out the best flavor in your meat or fish. You can prepare them ahead of time and take them with you, or you can mix them up as you need them.

Basil Oil

MAKES 1 CUP

2 tablespoons sea salt

1½ cups fresh basil leaves

1 cup extra-virgin olive oil

Bring a pot of water to a boil, add the salt, and make an ice-water bath (see tip, page 47).

Blanch the basil in the boiling water for 15 seconds, just until it is bright green and wilted. Drain and place the basil in the ice-water bath. Remove the basil immediately and dry on paper towels, gently squeezing out any water.

In a blender, process the oil and basil until smooth. Strain through a fine sieve, discarding the solids and store in a tightly covered container for up to 2 weeks.

Thyme Oil

MAKES 1 CUP

1 cup canola oil

1 bunch of fresh thyme

In a small saucepan, bring the oil and thyme to a simmer over medium heat and cook for 1 minute. Allow to cool slightly in the pan, then transfer the thyme oil to a glass container to cool completely. Strain the oil, discarding the thyme, and transfer into another clean glass container. Cover tightly. The oil can be stored in the refrigerator for up to 2 weeks.

Rosemary Oil

MAKES 1 CUP

In a small saucepan, heat the rosemary and oil on low heat until the aroma is released, 3 to 4 minutes. Allow to cool in the pan for a minute or two, then transfer to a heat-proof glass container and let cool completely. Allow the rosemary to steep in the oil at room temperature for 2 hours, then cover tightly and refrigerate for 2 days.

Before using, bring the oil back to room temperature and strain through a sieve, discarding the rosemary leaves. The oil can be stored refrigerated in a tightly covered container for up to 2 weeks.

½ cup finely chopped fresh rosemary leaves

1 cup canola oil

NOTE: The oil must be prepared at least 2 days ahead.

Ginger Oil

Use in a lively vinaigrette for Fancy Sweet Corn and Lobster Salad (opposite and page 164) or Aux Délices signature orzo salad (page 157).

MAKES 2¾ CUPS

¾ pound fresh ginger, thinly sliced (a scant 3 cups)

3 cups canola oil

In a medium saucepan, bring the ginger and canola oil to a boil over medium heat. Immediately remove from the heat and allow to cool to room temperature. Transfer to a glass container, cover, and refrigerate. To use, strain the amount of oil you want through a fine strainer, leaving the remainder in the jar with the ginger.

The oil will keep in the refrigerator for up to 2 weeks.

NOTE: The oil must be prepared at least 1 day ahead.

Herb Blend for Poultry and Lamb

MAKES ENOUGH TO SEASON 10 TO 12 CHICKEN BREASTS OR LAMB CHOPS

2 tablespoons curry powder

2 tablespoons ground cumin

1 tablespoon ground ginger

1 teaspoon cayenne pepper

1 tablespoon ground allspice

In a small bowl, stir together all of the ingredients. Store in an airtight container.

To use, rub the spice mixture over chicken or lamb and cover with plastic wrap. Let the meat marinate in the refrigerator for at least 2 hours. Season with salt and pepper before cooking.

Herb Blend for Fish

MAKES ENOUGH FOR 10 MEDIUM FILLETS

This rub works best on meaty fish like salmon, tuna, and swordfish.

In a small bowl, stir together all of the ingredients. Store in an airtight container.

To use, rub the spice mixture on the fish fillets and cover with plastic wrap. Let the fish marinate in the refrigerator for a few hours before cooking.

1 tablespoon ground cumin

2 tablespoons crushed coriander seed

2 tablespoons crushed fennel seed

1 teaspoon ground allspice

Lemon-Thyme Blend

Drizzle the chicken, meat, or fish on all sides with the oil. Generously sprinkle with the lemon peels, thyme, and pepper. Cover with plastic wrap and refrigerate for a few hours before cooking.

Canola oil

Lemon peels

Fresh thyme leaves

Freshly ground black pepper

MARINADES AND VINAIGRETTES

T hese marinades all use fresh ingredients, most of which you're likely to have on hand. They all work well with fish and poultry, and the Provençal Herb Marinade is especially good with lamb and steak. Don't worry about specific quantities—just be sure to generously cover the meat, poultry, or fish with the ingredients. They are invaluable time savers; just season your meat or fish right before you go to bed, so that next day's dinner is marinating while you're having a relaxing day.

At its most basic, a vinaigrette is a simple combination of ingredients: an acid such as vinegar or lemon juice, oil, and salt and pepper for seasoning. As with any preparation that straightforward, you'll find that the quality of vinegar and oil you use really makes a big difference in the resulting flavor. Likewise, the choice of vinegar makes a big enough difference in flavor that when we're at home, we can have up to five different vinaigrettes in the fridge that we use to dress different kinds of dishes. Debra's signature Sherry Shallot Vinaigrette is a good choice for every day, especially drizzled over a simple green salad. The delicate flavor of the Champagne Vinaigrette is perfect to use with seafood-based recipes, and the bracing Ginger Vinaigrette works well with any Asian-inspired dish and with rich beef or lobster dishes.

It goes against our summer minimalist grain to propose a wardrobe of five different vinaigrettes for our summer house, and when we go away, we usually pick two and work with them. But if you're the bring-all-the-shoes-I-might-possibly-need kind of traveler, we certainly wanted to give the option of having them all at your disposal.

The vinaigrettes can be stored in the refrigerator for up to two weeks.

Soy, Ginger, and Lime Marinade

MAKES 3 CUPS

The refreshing flavors of Asia are always a good choice in warmer weather, and this easy marinade packs a bracing punch. While it isn't necessary to roast the limes before juicing, heat causes them to give up much more juice, so you may need to use one or two extra if you skip that step. These three flavors are a natural marriage that works well with beef, chicken, and meaty fish like swordfish or tuna.

4 limes

2 cups soy sauce

⅓ pound ginger, peeled and thinly sliced

1 cup sliced scallions (white and green parts)

2 tablespoons honey

Preheat the oven to 350 °F.

Place the whole limes on a small baking tray and roast for 10 to 12 minutes, until the skins have softened. Set aside to cool.

In a medium bowl, combine the soy sauce, ginger, scallions, and honey. When the limes have cooled, cut them in half and squeeze to extract as much juice as possible. Stir the lime juice into the soy mixture until well blended. Drizzle the chicken, beef, or fish with enough marinade to coat and refrigerate for a few hours.

The marinade will keep in the refrigerator for up to 2 weeks.

Provençal Herb Marinade

This aromatic marinade works especially well with lamb and beef.

Canola oil

Sliced garlic cloves

Fresh rosemary leaves, coarsely chopped

Fresh thyme leaves, coarsely chopped

Herbes de Provence

Drizzle the meat on all sides with oil. Generously sprinkle with the remaining ingredients. Cover with plastic wrap and refrigerate for a few hours before cooking.

Lemon Vinaigrette

MAKES 2 CUPS

½ cup freshly squeezed lemon juice (from 2 large lemons)

1 teaspoon salt

1¾ cups extra-virgin olive oil

Freshly ground black pepper

In a small bowl, whisk the lemon juice and salt together until the salt dissolves. Slowly whisk in the oil until the dressing is well blended. Season with pepper.

Champagne Vinaigrette

MAKES 2 CUPS

In a small bowl, whisk the vinegar and salt together until the salt dissolves. Slowly whisk in the oil until the dressing is well blended. Season with pepper.

½ cup champagne vinegar

1 teaspoon sea salt

1½ cups extra-virgin olive oil

Freshly ground black pepper, to taste

Sherry Shallot Vinaigrette

MAKES 1½ CUPS

In a medium bowl, whisk the shallots, salt, and vinegar together until the salt dissolves. Slowly whisk in the oil until the dressing is well blended. Season with pepper.

¼ cup finely diced shallots (4 large)

¾ teaspoon sea salt

⅓ cup sherry vinegar

1 cup extra-virgin olive oil

Freshly ground black pepper, to taste

Sun-Dried Tomato and Basil Vinaigrette

MAKES 1⅓ CUPS

Place the sun-dried tomatoes in a small bowl. Pour the boiling water over the dried tomatoes to soften, 10 to 15 minutes. Remove the tomatoes, reserving the tomato water.

In a blender or food processor, combine the tomatoes, basil, garlic, vinegar, and 6 tablespoons of the tomato water or plain water and pulse until smooth. With the motor on low, slowly add the oil and blend until the dressing is well blended. Season with the salt and pepper.

NOTE: If you use tomatoes that are packed in oil, skip the first step of rehydrating.

½ cup sun-dried tomato halves, coarsely chopped (see Note)

1 cup boiling water

½ cup (packed) basil leaves

1 garlic clove

2 tablespoons plus 1 teaspoon red wine vinegar or balsamic vinegar

1 cup extra-virgin olive oil

½ teaspoon sea salt

Freshly ground black pepper, to taste

Ginger Vinaigrette

MAKES ⅔ CUP

In a small bowl, whisk together the vinegar and salt until the salt dissolves. Slowly whisk in the oil until the dressing is well blended. Season with pepper.

2 tablespoons champagne vinegar

¼ teaspoon sea salt

⅔ cup Ginger Oil (page 27)

Freshly ground black pepper, to taste

Summer Coolers and Finger Foods

We can't think of a better way to lengthen a relaxing afternoon than enjoying a cool pitcher of lemonade on the porch or a blenderful of daiquiris poolside. Chilled bottles of soda and beer are always a quick and easy choice for an impromptu picnic, but when unexpected company drops by, we think that it's just as simple to squeeze a bunch of lemons or purée some watermelon to mix up the thirst-quenching drinks or the fancy cocktails you'll find on the following pages. Cocktail nibbles often mean a bag of chips, a bowl of Goldfish crackers, and some packaged hummus. While we enjoy those, we like to round out the spread with one or two impressive finger foods, most of which can be pulled together in the time it takes you to shake, stir, and sip your cooler of the day. A tray of black-olive tapenade hors d'oeuvres, lobster cakes, or charred pesto shrimp will taste even better if you eat them as the sun sets.

COOLERS—STRAIGHT UP

These easy summer drink recipes are fresh, healthy thirst quenchers. Have someone help squeeze the lemons and limes while you search for the largest pitcher you can find. At our houses, vacation or not, we have at least one pitcher in the refrigerator at all times! For a more festive presentation, add a cup of raspberries to the pitcher of lemonade, or about 6 raspberries per glass.

Fresh-Squeezed Lemonade

MAKES A GENEROUS QUART

The mint syrup is a sweet and refreshing balance to the tart lemons.

In a medium pitcher, combine all of the ingredients and stir. Chill and serve ice cold.

½ cup freshly squeezed lemon juice (from 2 to 3 lemons)

¼ cup Simple Syrup (below) or Mint Syrup (page 77)

1 quart water

1 lemon, sliced in thin rounds, for garnish (optional)

SIMPLE SYRUP

Simple syrup dissolves readily in cold drinks, and we like to serve a little pitcher of it with iced tea so everyone can sweeten his or her own to taste.

MAKES 1¼ CUPS

1 cup water

2 cups sugar

In a saucepan, bring the water and sugar to a boil over high heat. Boil for 1 minute, stirring to dissolve the sugar completely. Remove from the heat and cool to room temperature.

Store in the refrigerator for up to 2 weeks.

Fresh-Squeezed Limeade

MAKES A GENEROUS QUART

The clean, revitalizing flavor of lime is a nice alternative to the more traditional lemonade.

In a medium pitcher, combine all of the ingredients and stir. Chill and serve ice cold.

½ cup freshly squeezed lime juice (from 5 limes)

¼ cup Simple Syrup (opposite)

1 quart water

Fruit Purées and Coolers

SERVES ABOUT 8

Ripe summer fruits, simply puréed and mixed with seltzer, make delicious, naturally sweet summer drinks. We've suggested some of our favorites, but feel free to try any fruit you like.

Place the fruit in a blender and process until smooth.

To make a strawberry or mango cooler, place 3 tablespoons of the purée in a tall glass and top with 8 ounces of seltzer. For a sweeter drink simply add more purée.

To make the nectarine cooler, top 3 tablespoon of purée with $1/2$ cup of orange juice and $1/2$ cup of seltzer.

Stir and add some ice cubes. Finish all of the drinks with a squeeze of lemon or lime.

18 to 20 medium strawberries, hulled, *or* 1 mango, peeled, pitted, and sliced, *or* 2 nectarines, peeled, pitted, and quartered

2 quarts seltzer, as needed

1 quart fresh orange juice (for nectarine drinks only)

1 lemon or lime, cut in wedges

COOLERS WITH A KICK

While summer quenchers like a gin and tonic or a cold beer are an easy way to coast through the cocktail hour, there are other festive cocktails that we're sure were invented just for hot-weather sipping. We've included some classics, along with a few drinks inspired by our favorite watering holes.

Bloody Mary—Saratoga Style

SERVES 4 TO 5

This classic dates back to Paris in the 1920s and it finally found its way to New York in 1933 when its originator, Pete Petiot, began working at the famed King Cole Bar at the St. Regis Hotel. We love the eye-watering spiciness that horseradish adds, but for a more mellow batch, halve the horseradish and go easy on the Tabasco.

In a large pitcher, mix together the tomato juice, Worcestershire, horseradish, celery salt, pepper, Tabasco, and vodka. Stir until all of the ingredients are mixed well. Just before serving, add the lime juice. Pour into tall glasses filled with ice. Garnish with a celery rib and a lime wedge.

4 cups good-quality tomato juice

4 tablespoons Worcestershire sauce

2 tablespoons prepared horseradish

2 teaspoons celery salt

1½ teaspoons freshly ground black pepper

2 teaspoons Tabasco sauce

8 ounces vodka

Juice of ½ lime

Celery ribs, cleaned and trimmed, for garnish

Lime wedges, for garnish

Citrus Martini

On a hot summer's evening, martini lovers will appreciate this refreshing variation on the classic. To get an icy cold drink, shake the cocktail shaker vigorously so that slivers of ice break off and are poured into the glasses with the liquid.

1 ounce Cointreau

4 ounces Absolut Mandrin or Absolut Citron vodka

1 ounce freshly squeezed orange juice

1 ounce freshly squeezed lemon juice

Orange zest, for garnish (see Note)

In a large shaker filled with ice, add all of the ingredients except the orange rind. Shake very vigorously. Pour the mixture through a cocktail strainer into well-chilled martini glasses.

NOTE: To make the orange garnish, use a good-quality zester to slice a piece of orange zest $1/2$ inch wide by about 6 inches long (vegetable peelers and paring knives work well too). Wrap the strip lengthwise around a cocktail stirrer, wooden spoon, or chopstick. Hold the strip in place for a minute, then slide it off. You'll have a beautiful orange "spiral" to garnish your cocktail.

Watermelon Cooler

SERVES 6

Geralyn and her husband were inspired to make this delicious concoction after they tried it at a favorite bistro in SoHo called L'Orange Bleue. Enjoyed straight up by the kids and spiked with vodka for the adults, it's been a resounding hit when we entertain. The drink is equally good when paired with rum or tequila (our hands-down favorite). You can make this by the glass or by the pitcher.

½ medium seedless watermelon (5 pounds)

2 cups lemonade, homemade (page 36) or good-quality prepared

12 ounces vodka, tequila, or rum (optional)

Cut the watermelon flesh into chunks and, working in batches, purée in a blender until liquified. Strain through a fine sieve to remove the pulp; you should have about 4 cups of juice. Combine the watermelon juice and the lemonade in a 2-quart pitcher.

To make individual cocktails, fill a shaker with ice. Add 1 cup of the watermelon–lemonade mixture and 2 ounces of alcohol. Shake vigorously. Strain into a tall glass filled with ice or a chilled martini glass.

Peach Mango Daiquiri

SERVES 4

Even if your summer house is an urban rooftop, don't despair. Mix up a batch of these, slip on your flip-flops, and crank up the Calypso music—a few drinks later you'll be doing the limbo and fantasizing you're on a fabulous island in the Caribbean. Mango juice and peach nectar are easy to find these days, even in suburban food markets, but a health food or specialty shop is a sure bet if you strike out at the market. Mount Gay is our rum of choice for daiquiris.

5 cups ice

6 ounces amber rum

¾ cup mango juice

¾ cup peach nectar

1 cup freshly squeezed lime juice

Fresh peach slices, for garnish

In a blender, combine the ice, rum, and all three juices. The blender will be quite full, so place a towel over the top and hold it while processing. Purée until the mixture is smooth and creamy. Serve in chilled martini glasses and garnish with a peach slice.

Patrick's Perfect Margarita

SERVES 4

The margarita is a bartender's ode to summer. Mix up a big pitcher, add a porch, a sunset, and Deb's Best-Ever Guacamole (page 58), and you can save yourself the airfare to Puerto Vallarta. To salt glass rims, simply run a wedge of lime around the top quarter inch of the glass and dip it into a saucer of sea salt.

6 ounces tequila (a scant 5 jiggers)

2 ounces Cointreau

2 ounces Simple Syrup (page 36)

6 ounces fresh lime juice

Sea salt, for garnish (optional)

Lime wedges, for garnish

Fill a large cocktail shaker with ice. Add the tequila, Cointreau, syrup, and lime juice and shake vigorously. Serve in chilled martini glasses, with or without salted rims, and garnished with lime wedges.

> **Tip:** Ten limes yield about one cup of juice. Look for limes with a smooth (not dimpled) skin; they're juicier. Invest in a good-quality hand juicer if you like margaritas; you'll thank us when you're ready for that second round of drinks and you don't have to squeeze a dozen more limes by hand!

Mint Royale

SERVES 1

This delicious apéritif, inspired by the signature Verbena Royale cocktail at Manhattan's Verbena Restaurant, calls for Lillet Blanc, a blend of wine, brandy, fruits, and herbs. Light and fruity, with a dry finish, Lillet also tastes great served on its own over ice, with an orange slice for garnish.

1 teaspoon Mint Syrup (page 77)

2 tablespoons Lillet Blanc

5 ounces sparkling wine or champagne

Orange zest, for garnish

Pour the syrup and the Lillet in a champagne flute. Top with champagne and garnish with an orange "spiral" (see Note, page 40).

> **Tip: The Impromptu Bartender**
Don't worry if you don't have all the proper tools of the trade to mix up your cocktails— we've improvised with all kinds of things!

- If your summer house bar doesn't stock a cocktail shaker, try using two oversized plastic glasses (a quick trip to Taco Bell or McDonald's for one large and one medium soda and you're there). They might not fit perfectly inside one another, so we suggest shaking over the sink.

- While a citrus zester is really nice because it makes zests of perfect width, a good old vegetable peeler will give you a nice peel that can be split lengthwise to make two.

- No large pitchers handy? This is a tough one, but plastic jugs work and so do large bowls and a ladle.

WHAT EXACTLY IS A JIGGER?

A jigger is a bar measurement that determines how much liquor should go in one drink. The standard bar pour is 1¼ ounces. We've used the correct bar lingo in our drink recipes, which calls for ingredients in jiggers and ounces, but when you're mixing up a pitcher of Bloody Marys or limeade, it can get to be a bit of a chore to do all the math in your head. Below is a table of liquid measurements and their equivalents that will help to make things easier on the designated bartender.

1 ounce = 2 tablespoons
1¼ ounces = 1 jigger
2 ounces = ¼ cup
4 ounces = ½ cup
8 ounces = 1 cup
16 ounces = 2 cups or 1 pint
2 pints = 1 quart

Cocktail parties should be more about the people than the food, and making trays of fussy little mouthfuls can be the daunting detail that sends even the best host or hostess over the edge. But finger foods like these are easy— and fun—to prepare.

Sweet and Spicy Nuts

MAKES 7 CUPS

The ultimate in cocktail nibbles, these nuts can be made ahead and stored in a tightly sealed plastic container. At cocktail time you'll have something to snack on that requires nothing more than setting out a bowl.

¼ cup canola oil

1 teaspoon cayenne pepper

1 tablespoon plus 1 teaspoon ground cumin

7 cups mixed unsalted nuts, such as walnuts, pecans, almonds, pistachios and hazelnuts

3 tablespoons sugar

3 teaspoons sea salt

Preheat the oven to 350°F.

In a small saucepan, heat the oil, cayenne, and cumin until just warm.

In a large bowl, mix the nuts and the spicy oil, tossing until the nuts are evenly coated.

In a small bowl, mix together the sugar and salt. Add it to the nuts and toss to mix well.

Spread the nuts on a baking sheet and bake them for 18 to 20 minutes, until golden brown, stirring them once or twice.

Remove the nuts from the oven and allow them to cool to room temperature. Store the nuts in a resealable plastic bag or a plastic container with a tight lid; they'll keep for 2 to 3 weeks.

Roasted Eggplant Crostini

MAKES 1 CUP TAPENADE OR 18 TO 20 HORS D'OEUVRES

A "flavor sponge," eggplant melds perfectly with any ingredients you pair with it. This recipe is truly Provençal—a few olives, a sprinkling of herbs, and you have a tasty hors d'oeuvre. Serve it with your favorite brand of hummus, some pita bread, and a bowl of olives for a Mediteranean-inspired cocktail hour.

1 small eggplant, halved lengthwise

¼ cup plus 3 tablespoons extra-virgin olive oil

Sea salt and freshly ground black pepper

1 teaspoon herbes de Provence

10 black olives, pitted

1 small baguette, sliced in ¼-inch rounds

Preheat the oven to 350°F.

Slash the cut surfaces of the eggplant in a crosshatch pattern and drizzle with 3 tablespoons of the olive oil. Season the eggplant with salt, pepper, and the herbes de Provence and place on a baking sheet, cut sides up.

Bake for 40 to 50 minutes, until the flesh is very soft. Remove from the oven and allow to cool to room temperature.

Scoop out the eggplant flesh and place it in a blender or food processor with the olives. Process until the mixture is well blended and smooth.

Preheat the broiler.

Place the baguette slices on a baking sheet, brush them with the remaining ¹/₄ cup of olive oil, lightly season with salt and pepper, and broil until golden brown. Spread 1 teaspoon of the eggplant mixture on each crouton. Arrange the crostini on a platter and serve.

Tomato and Black Olive Bruschetta on Garlic Toasts

MAKES 2 CUPS OR 20 TO 24 HORS D'OEUVRES

This distinctive variation on the standard tomato and basil version is one of the best ways we know to use all of those extra beefsteak tomatoes that got ripe on the sill at the same time! If you can't be bothered with blanching the tomatoes to make them easy to peel, just leave the skins on—sweet, ripe tomatoes taste great either way.

¾ pound (about 3 medium) ripe tomatoes

4 tablespoons extra-virgin olive oil

¼ teaspoon sea salt

⅛ teaspoon freshly ground black pepper

1½ teaspoons balsamic vinegar

20 large black olives, pitted and chopped

1 tablespoon chopped fresh thyme

1 clove Roasted Garlic (page 19), optional

1 small baguette, cut into ¼-inch rounds

Make an ice-water bath (see Note).

Meanwhile, bring a medium pot of water to a boil. Core the tomatoes and cut an X in the bottom of each with the tip of a knife. Blanch the tomatoes in the boiling water for about 10 seconds, then remove the tomatoes from the water with tongs and place in the bowl of ice water.

Drain the tomatoes, then peel and cut them into quarters. Remove the seeds and ribs with a sharp knife and discard. Each tomato will yield four "petals" of flesh. Cut each petal into thin strips and then into a small dice and place in a medium bowl.

Stir in 2 tablespoons of the oil, the salt, pepper, vinegar, olives, and thyme. Toss gently.

Preheat the broiler, or prepare the grill.

If you are using the roasted garlic, mash the garlic with the remaining 2 tablespoons of oil. Brush the baguette slices with the oil, lightly season with salt and pepper, and place the slices on a baking sheet if using the broiler. Toast the slices until golden brown, then set aside to cool.

Spoon 2 teaspoons of the tomato–olive mixture onto each bread slice and arrange on a festive platter to serve.

NOTE: We call for an ice-water bath in a lot of our recipes. It's really nothing more than a bowl of ice water that's used to "shock" or stop the cooking of vegetables so that they retain their vibrant color and texture. It is very easy to do (see tip), and we think it really makes a difference in the resulting flavor, but if it doesn't fit in with your summer house state of mind, just skip this step.

> **Tip:** To make the ice-water bath, select a bowl large enough to accommodate the vegetables or seafood you're preparing. Fill the bowl with ice and water. When the vegetables are cooked properly, transfer them to the bath and allow them to cool. It is important to remove the veggies or seafood as soon as they are cooled down, usually no more than 2 minutes, so that they don't get waterlogged.

Herbed Goat Cheese Spread

MAKES 3 CUPS

We love this goat cheese spread smeared on almost any kind of bread that's been stuffed with leftover grilled veggies or sliced roast beef or lamb. Or serve it with raw vegetables, toasted baguette rounds, or crackers for instant hors d'oeuvres.

1 tablespoon finely chopped fresh chives

1 tablespoon finely chopped fresh flat-leaf parsley

1 tablespoon finely chopped fresh thyme

1 tablespoon finely chopped fresh dill

8 ounces fresh goat cheese, at room temperature

4 ounces cream cheese, at room temperature

½ cup Crème Fraîche (page 22) or sour cream

In a medium bowl, mix all of the ingredients until well combined. Cover with plastic wrap and store in the refrigerator until ready to serve. The spread will keep in the refrigerator for up to 2 weeks.

Tapenade Two Ways

The outdoor markets in every little town in Provence offer tapenades—usually at least five different kinds—for sale from huge earthenware crocks. Here are two of Debra's favorites: They make a healthy alternative to butter at the dinner table, add an interesting layer of flavor to sandwiches, and are a flavorful nibble served on crackers when friends drop in unexpectedly.

ZUCCHINI TAPENADE

MAKES 2 CUPS

Can't pass up these inexpensive beauties, found in overwhelming quantities at every farm stand come mid-July? As an alternative to throwing zucchini on the grill, try transforming it into this flavorful spread for toast points or slices of baguette. The roasted garlic and capers add a bold Mediterranean zip.

2 medium zucchini, ends trimmed and cut into small pieces

1 anchovy fillet

¼ cup extra-virgin olive oil

4 cloves Roasted Garlic (page 19)

2 teaspoons capers, drained

Sea salt and freshly ground black pepper, to taste

Place the zucchini, anchovy, oil, garlic, and capers in a food processor or blender and process just until chopped fine. Don't over-process or the mixture will get watery. Season with salt and pepper.

BLACK OLIVE TAPENADE

MAKES 1¼ CUPS

Use any good-quality olives from the Mediterranean for this spread. At Graham's, Geralyn's restaurant in Saratoga Springs, New York, they serve this in place of butter with their house-made breads; Geralyn especially likes it when the kitchen mixes up a batch with both green and black olives.

2 cups pitted kalamata olives, or French green olives

2 tablespoons capers, drained

4 cloves Roasted Garlic (page 19)

4 anchovy fillets

¼ cup extra-virgin olive oil

Freshly ground black pepper, to taste

Combine all the ingredients in a blender or food processor. Blend on low until the mixture is smooth. If using a blender, stop occasionally and stir the mixture. When the mixture is almost blended, pulse to achieve a smooth consistency.

Charred Pesto Shrimp

SERVES 4 TO 6

The smell of fresh herbs at the outdoor market—or better yet, in your own herb garden—is one of summer's great joys. Combine your favorites in an herbed pesto, made without the cheese or nuts so that the delicate flavors of the herbs stand front and center. Paired with sweet shrimp, it makes for a very versatile dish that can be used as a great hors d'oeuvre, a light appetizer, or a main course. For an easy summer pasta dish, cook linguine or angel hair, toss it with some leftover pesto, and top with the grilled shrimp and a garnish of chopped fresh basil or parsley.

1 cup (packed) fresh basil leaves

¼ cup fresh tarragon leaves

¼ cup fresh cilantro leaves

¼ cup fennel fronds (optional)

¼ cup fresh chives

¼ cup flat-leaf parsley

1 tablespoon grated lemon zest

¾ cup extra-virgin olive oil

½ teaspoon sea salt

Freshly ground black pepper, to taste

24 jumbo shrimp, peeled and deveined (see Note)

Roughly chop the basil leaves and place in a blender or a food processor. Add the tarragon, cilantro, fennel fronds, chives, parsley, lemon zest, oil, salt, and pepper. Process until smooth. You should have about 1 cup of pesto; it will have a somewhat loose, saucelike consistency.

Place half the pesto in a large bowl, add the shrimp, and toss to coat thoroughly.

Prepare a medium-hot grill.

Grill the shrimp for 2 minutes; using tongs, turn and grill the other side for 2 more minutes. Transfer the cooked shrimp to a platter and drizzle with the remaining pesto. Serve warm or at room temperature skewered with toothpicks for easy handling.

NOTE: If you buy smaller shrimp, place them on a skewer before grilling so they don't fall through the grill rack into the fire.

Rosemary-Skewered Chicken

MAKES 20 HORS D'OEUVRES

Look like a pro without spending a lot of time in the kitchen with these pretty rosemary-skewered hors d'oeuvres. They have never failed to impress our guests, no matter what the season.

1 pound boneless, skinless chicken breast, cut into twenty 1½-inch chunks

2 teaspoons chopped fresh rosemary

Grated zest of 1 lemon

2 teaspoons freshly squeezed lemon juice

½ cup canola oil

Sea salt and freshly ground black pepper, to taste

20 rosemary sprigs, or long toothpicks

In a medium bowl, mix together the chicken, chopped rosemary, lemon zest and juice, 6 tablespoons of the oil, salt, and pepper. Cover with plastic wrap and refrigerate for at least 2 hours.

In a medium sauté pan, heat the remaining 2 tablespoons of oil until smoking. Sear the chicken pieces for 1½ minutes on each side, or until cooked through. Transfer the chicken to a platter. Remove some of the leaves from the end of each rosemary sprig, then insert the sprig (or a toothpick) into each chunk of chicken.

Bar Harbor Lobster Cakes

MAKES 12 HORS D'OEUVRES OR 4 APPETIZER PORTIONS

Any of our summer sojourns to the coast absolutely require a trip to the local lobster pound for a traditional home-cooked lobster feast. The next day, we make leftovers into mini lobster cakes to accompany cocktails. These are so good it's worth throwing another lobster or two into the pot to ensure there will be some sweet lobster meat left over. Serve the lobster cakes with remoulade dipping sauce.

In a medium bowl, mix together the mayonnaise, mustard, tarragon, capers, and lemon zest. Stir in the lobster and 1½ cups fresh bread crumbs, mixing well.

Make 12 bite-size cakes or four 2-inch-wide cakes, dividing the mixture evenly. Cover them with plastic wrap and refrigerate for about 1 hour.

Spread some Wondra flour or bread crumbs on a plate. Dredge the cakes on both sides, pressing the bread crumbs to adhere them.

Preheat the oven to 375°F. if you are serving the larger, appetizer-size cakes.

Place the oil in a sauté pan and heat over a high flame until almost smoking. Reduce heat to medium and add the lobster cakes, cooking for about 1 minute on each side or until the coating is golden brown. Bite-size cakes are ready to serve and eat; transfer larger cakes to a baking sheet and bake until cooked through, about 18 to 20 minutes.

½ cup Fresh Mayonnaise (page 21), or good-quality prepared mayonnaise

1 tablespoon Dijon mustard

1 tablespoon chopped fresh tarragon

1 tablespoon capers, rinsed and roughly chopped

½ teaspoon grated lemon zest

½ pound cooked lobster meat (see page 139 for quantity), cut into small dice

1½ cups fresh bread crumbs

½ teaspoon sea salt

Freshly ground black pepper

Wondra flour or additional bread crumbs, for coating

2 cups canola oil, or enough to reach halfway up the cake when frying

Remoulade Sauce (opposite)

> **Tip:** To make 1½ cups of fresh bread crumbs, remove the crusts from 5 to 6 slices white bread and place in a blender or food processor. Pulse until fine.

Remoulade Sauce

MAKES 1¼ CUPS

This traditional French sauce is really just a souped-up tartar that also makes a nice dressing for cold poached lobster, shrimp, or beef filet. Use any leftovers to whip up a classic celery root salad or to dress your favorite coleslaw recipe. The dressing can be kept in the refrigerator for up to 5 days.

1 cup Fresh Mayonnaise (page 21) or good-quality prepared mayonnaise

2 tablespoons chopped cornichons or good-quality gherkins

1 tablespoon chopped capers

2 tablespoons chopped fresh tarragon

Freshly ground black pepper, to taste

In a medium bowl, mix together the mayonnaise, cornichons, capers, tarragon and pepper. Cover with plastic wrap and refrigerate until ready to serve.

Ginger-Spiked Tuna Tartare

MAKES 2 DOZEN HORS D'OEUVRES OR 4 APPETIZER SERVINGS

You're the only one who needs to know that this impressive, restaurant-quality canapé takes only 5 minutes to make. The tartare can be served on slices of cucumber or toasted baguette rounds as an hors d'oeuvre, or mounded on a small bed of greens that have been drizzled with ginger oil and rice wine vinegar for a light first course.

½ pound sushi-quality tuna

1 tablespoon Ginger Oil (page 27)

¼ teaspoon wasabi powder

¼ teaspoon sesame seeds

1 teaspoon finely chopped fresh cilantro

¼ to ½ teaspoon sea salt

Freshly ground black pepper, to taste

Cut the tuna into ¼-inch slices, then cut lengthwise into strips and across into ¼-inch dice. Place in a small bowl. Add the ginger oil, wasabi, sesame seeds, cilantro, ¼ teaspoon of salt, and pepper. Stir to combine, then set aside for a few minutes to let the flavors develop. Taste and add a bit more salt if necessary.

Picnics
and
More

Our earliest exposure to alfresco dining with portable foods was probably the tailgating parties and hunt meets that are popular throughout New Jersey, where we both grew up. These tend to be a bit more elaborate than simple picnics under a tree, so it's not surprising that as adults, we still enjoy the beautiful blanket, candles, and real wineglasses kind of picnics. ⬤ That doesn't mean we don't look forward to spur-of-the-moment eating adventures that include a terrific sandwich (we've included a whole list of our favorites, all made with leftovers from recipes in other chapters) and a piece of fruit. Scenery is just about as important as food to the picnic setting, and if you find a beautiful spot near the water or under the stars to spread your blanket, it's hard to go wrong. But we do think it's worth taking a bit of time in the morning to pack up a great spread. That way your day of bird-watching, bike riding, or lolling on the beach doesn't have to be punctuated by a stop at the hot dog stand or a granola bar on the go.

PICNIC POINTERS

Whoen planning your picnic, keep in mind where your movable feast will be and how long the food needs to hold before you eat it. In the warmer months, food safety is always an issue, and even foods that can be eaten at room temperature shouldn't remain outside the refrigerator for hours on end. We suggest you invest in a really good ice chest, and use the pretty picnic basket to tote your plates, glasses, and silverware.

ESSENTIALS

- Bread knife (for cheese and fruit, too)
- Corkscrew
- Small cutting board
- Trash bag
- Citronella candles or insect repellant, with lighter or matches

FOOD TIPS

- Store all of your food in a good ice chest.
- Use last night's leftovers to make cool salads and creative sandwiches (see page 61).
- Sturdy, precooked foods like sliced meats and poached seafood make good picnic fare.
- Mix store-bought items—good deli mats, crusty rolls, and good-quality cheeses—with homemade condiments and accompaniments you have in your refrigerator.
- If you like sliced tomatoes and lettuce on sandwiches, pack them in plastic bags separate from your sandwiches; then, right before you're ready to eat, garnish your sandwich with the accompaniments so there's no soggy mess.
- Don't forget to pack up interesting drinks. Freeze lemonade or limeade (see pages 36 and 37) in a portable plastic jug the night before and it will be just right by the time you're ready to drink it.

Pack-and-Pour Chilled Nectarine Soup

SERVES 4

This healthy, sweet soup wins our vote for favorite take-to-the-beach lunch. The added plus is its versatility: Serve any leftovers the next day at breakfast with a side of Honey Nut Granola (page 84) or paired with your favorite salad for an elegant summer lunch. Kids love it as an anytime snack that can be poured into a thermos so it stays fresh and cold.

8 nectarines, pitted and diced

2½ cups orange juice

1 tablespoon sugar

1 sprig of fresh tarragon

1½ cups plain low-fat yogurt

In a large sauté pan with deep sides, bring the nectarines, orange juice, sugar, and tarragon to a boil. Reduce the heat to medium and simmer until the nectarines are very tender, 8 to 10 minutes.

Transfer the fruit mixture to a bowl and allow it to cool to room temperature. Stir in the yogurt.

Working in batches, purée the soup using a blender, food processor, or hand blender until smooth. Chill for at least 2 to 3 hours and serve cold.

Best-Ever Guacamole

MAKES 2½ CUPS

Guacamole is one of summer's quintessential pleasures. After experimenting with a few recipes, this fairly classic version turned out to be our favorite, and it takes all of about 10 minutes to make. For a spicier dip, add the Tabasco and more jalapeño. Pair it with some tortilla chips and Patrick's Perfect Margaritas (page 42) for an effortless transition into dinner.

With the tip of a knife, score the avocado flesh and scoop it into a medium bowl. Mash with a fork or potato masher until fairly smooth. Stir in the remaining ingredients, mixing well but gently, and serve immediately.

3 ripe Hass avocados, halved lengthwise and pit removed

½ medium onion, finely diced

1 small tomato, seeded and finely diced

2 tablespoons finely chopped fresh cilantro

½ large jalapeño, seeded and finely diced

¼ teaspoon ground cumin

Juice of 1 lime

1 teaspoon sea salt

1 dash of Tabasco sauce (optional)

Summer's Best Gazpacho

SERVES 6 TO 8

There are different philosophies on gazpacho. Debra prefers the slightly chunky version you get using a food processor, while Geralyn likes a thick soup with finer vegetable bits (throw everything in a blender and pulse). Whichever you prefer, ladle this spicy, healthy soup into a thermos for easy toting to your favorite picnic spot. For fancier occasions, we add three or four large cooked shrimp to each serving. (Photograph on page 54)

In a medium nonreactive bowl, mix all of the ingredients together. Working in batches using a blender or food processor, pulse the mixture once or twice so that it is blended but the vegetables still have texture. Taste for seasoning and adjust if necessary.

Transfer to a glass bowl or plastic container and refrigerate until ready to serve.

1 large red bell pepper, cored, seeds and ribs removed, cut into medium dice

1 cucumber, peeled, trimmed, and cut into medium dice

1 medium red onion, cut into medium dice

2 celery stalks, split lengthwise and cut into medium dice

6 fresh leaves basil, sliced

2 tablespoons coarsely chopped fresh cilantro leaves

½ jalapeño pepper, seeded and minced

4 cups good-quality tomato juice

1 tablespoon balsamic vinegar

1½ teaspoons sea salt

Cold Roasted Filet of Beef with Watercress Sauce

SERVES 10 TO 12

New Jersey is known for its horse country and hunt meets. Both of us loved to go each year, and the extravagant tailgating parties were as much fun as the races. The cold filet of beef was a favored dish at these parties—it is easy to prepare and serve for all kinds of outdoor eating adventures. Serve the beef with Watercress Sauce or, for more casual gatherings, with Provençal Mustard (page 69).

5- to 6-pound beef tenderloin, cleaned and silver skin removed

10 shallots, peeled and thinly sliced

½ cup canola oil

4 tablespoons fresh rosemary leaves, roughly chopped

4 tablespoons fresh thyme leaves, roughly chopped

8 garlic cloves, thinly sliced

Sea salt and freshly ground black pepper, to taste

5 sprigs fresh rosemary

Watercress Sauce (opposite)

Place the beef in a shallow dish and cover with the shallots, oil, rosemary, thyme, and garlic. Cover in plastic wrap, refrigerate, and marinate the meat overnight.

Remove the filet from the refrigerator and allow it to come to room temperature, about 1 hour. Remove any remaining garlic, shallots, and herbs from the meat. Season with salt and pepper on all sides.

Tuck the tip end under to make a uniformly thick piece of meat and tie the roast crosswise with kitchen twine every 2 inches, inserting the rosemary sprigs under the twine.

Prepare a medium-hot grill.

Grill the meat uncovered, turning a few times, until an instant-read thermometer reads 125°F. for medium rare, about 35 to 40 minutes.

Transfer the filet to a carving board and let it rest for 15 to 20 minutes. If you plan to serve the meat cold, wrap it in plastic and refrigerate.

When ready to serve, carve in ¹/₂-inch slices and serve with Watercress Sauce on the side.

Watercress Sauce

MAKES 2⅓ CUPS

This is also a good accompaniment to poached salmon and works well as a dip with raw vegetables.

In a blender or food processor, pulse the watercress until finely chopped. Add the crème fraîche, mayonnaise, salt, and pepper and process until smooth.

Transfer to a bowl or plastic container and refrigerate until ready to use. It will keep for up to 5 days.

2½ cups watercress, large stems removed (about 2 bunches)

½ cup Crème Fraîche (page 22) or sour cream

½ cup Fresh Mayonnaise (page 21), or good-quality prepared mayonnaise

½ teaspoon sea salt

Freshly ground black pepper, to taste

TURNING LEFTOVERS INTO A GREAT SANDWICH

Start with great bread. Slather on some of our summer spreads, such as the herbed goat cheese spread on page 47 or Provençal mustard (page 69). Pick your protein: leftover tuna, lamb, chicken, pork, or beef. Garnish with summer vegetables. It's that easy to go from ham and cheese on rye to a memorable lunch. Here are some favorite combos, in no particular order:

- **Filet of beef** (opposite) with arugula, tomato, balsamic-marinated onions (page 96) and Roquefort mustard (page 124)
- **Flank steak** (page 162), balsamic-marinated red onions (page 96), romaine, and vinaigrette of choice (pages 31–33)
- **Pork loin** (page 158) with apricot chutney, arugula, and honey mustard
- **Leg of lamb** (page 144), grilled Moroccan eggplant (page 129), oven-roasted tomatoes (page 97), and black olive tapenade (page 48) on pita

- **Crab salad** (page 62) on white bread topped with sprouts or baby lettuce
- **Barbecued chicken** (page 120) with Memorial Day Coleslaw (page 153)
- **Filet of beef** (page 60) and watercress sauce (above) on white bread
- **Leg of lamb** (page 144), roasted red peppers (page 96), and arugula
- **Roasted chicken** (page 136), lettuce, tomato, and Caesar dressing (page 149)
- **Fresh tuna** (page 123), greens, and Caesar dressing (page 149)

East Hampton Crab Salad

MAKES 4 APPETIZER SERVINGS OR 4 SANDWICHES

Yes, it's extravagant, but what are vacations for? When Debra rented a summer house in the Hamptons, this was one of her entertaining hits that visiting friends always requested. Take the extra minute or two to make homemade mayonnaise for this recipe and you'll love the fresh, delicate flavor that results. This can be served as a salad in a Bibb lettuce cup or on some sliced, vine-ripened tomatoes, but it also makes a delicious sandwich, served on white peasant bread topped with greens.

1 pound jumbo lump crab meat, picked over for cartilage

¼ cup finely diced red onion

¼ cup sliced scallions (white and green parts)

2 teaspoons chopped fresh tarragon

½ teaspoon finely chopped fresh mint

1 teaspoon grated lemon zest

¼ cup Fresh Mayonnaise (page 21), or good-quality prepared mayonnaise

3 teaspoons Dijon mustard

½ teaspoon sea salt

Freshly ground black pepper, to taste

In a medium bowl, combine the crab, onion, scallions, tarragon, mint, and lemon zest. In a small bowl stir together the mayonnaise and mustard. Add the mayo-mustard mixture to the crab and toss until the dressing evenly coats the salad. Season with the salt and pepper.

Cover with plastic wrap and refrigerate until ready to serve.

Corsican Orzo Salad

SERVES 4 TO 6

A hands-down winner at picnics and barbecues, this Greek-inspired pasta salad is tangy and full of clean flavor. It tastes even better served the next day, so it's a good choice to make ahead for a party. Double the recipe for easy-to-pack leftovers to take on a hike or to the beach.

Bring a medium-size pot of salted water to a boil over high heat. Add the orzo and cook according to package directions. Drain immediately and rinse with cold water.

In a large bowl, add the orzo, herbs, lemon juice and zest, and oil. Toss until well coated. Crumble the feta cheese into the bowl. Add the olives and toss again.

Sea salt

1 pound orzo (2⅔ cups)

1 tablespoon finely chopped fresh dill

1 tablespoon finely chopped fresh tarragon leaves

1 tablespoon finely chopped fresh flat-leaf parsley

1 tablespoon finely chopped fresh cilantro leaves

Zest and juice of 1 lemon

6 tablespoons extra-virgin olive oil

1½ cups feta cheese

15 French black or kalamata olives, pitted and roughly chopped

Niçoise Bean Salad

SERVES 6 TO 8

This pretty salad gets its Niçoise name from the preparations favored in the South of France, which typically include green beans, tomatoes, and garlic. Here the tomatoes are sun-dried and the garlic is roasted for an added intensity Be playful with your choice of beans if you have access to a few varieties; dragon beans, cranberry beans, and fava beans are other good alternatives to the ones we use here. If time is an issue, you can forgo the roasted garlic, but the salad is so much tastier with it that we suggest roasting some the night before.

1 pound green beans, ends trimmed

1 pound yellow wax beans, ends trimmed

12 cloves Roasted Garlic (page 19)

20 grape or cherry tomatoes, halved

¼ cup Sun-Dried Tomato and Basil Vinaigrette (page 33) or Sherry Shallot Vinaigrette (page 32)

1½ teaspoons sea salt

Freshly ground black pepper, to taste

Make an ice-water bath (see tip, page 47).

Bring a large pot of salted water to a boil. Add both kinds of beans, reduce the heat to medium, and cook for 3 to 4 minutes, until the beans are just tender. Drain and place in the bowl of ice water for a few minutes.

When the beans are cool, drain immediately and place them in a large bowl. Add the garlic, tomatoes, and vinaigrette and toss until mixed. Season with the salt and pepper.

Picnic Basket Fried Chicken

SERVES 4

Deep-fry? In the middle of summer? We know, but fried chicken holds great childhood memories of picnics by the sea or under the stars watching the Fourth of July fireworks. Cut up the chicken and marinate it overnight; the next day you can fry it (and heat up the kitchen) early in the day before it gets warm. Then you are good to go until the cooler evening hours.

2 pounds chicken pieces (breasts, legs, and thighs)

3 cups buttermilk

4 cups vegetable shortening, for frying

Sea salt and freshly ground black pepper

4 eggs, beaten

3 cups flour

With a cleaver or heavy knife, split the chicken breasts, then cut each breast half in half again.

Place the chicken pieces in a shallow container skin side down and pour the buttermilk over them. Cover with plastic wrap and marinate in the refrigerator for at least 6 hours or overnight if possible.

Preheat the oven to 375°F.

Remove the chicken from the buttermilk and season both sides with salt and pepper.

Place the beaten eggs and flour in separate shallow bowls. Dredge the chicken pieces first in the flour, then the egg, and then the flour again.

In a 12-inch sauté pan with deep sides, melt enough shortening so that it is 2 inches deep and heat the pan until the oil begins to smoke.

Fry the chicken for 2 minutes on each side, until the skin is golden brown. Transfer to a baking sheet and bake the chicken for 15 minutes, or until cooked through.

Serve warm immediately, or store in the refrigerator for the next day's picnic.

Cold Poached Salmon with Provençal Mustard

SERVES 4

Because salmon is a sturdy, steaklike fish that retains its pretty color and flavor at room temperature, it's the ideal choice for an al fresco entrée. We always toted a cooler of these sophisticated fillets to the concerts given by the New York Philharmonic in Central Park. Add French Country Potato Salad (page 101) and the Niçoise Bean Salad (page 65) for a truly elegant spread.

4 salmon fillets (6 ounces each)

Sea salt and finely ground black pepper

3 cups chicken stock, or low-sodium canned broth

Provençal Mustard (opposite)

Preheat the oven to 350°F.

Season the salmon fillets with salt and pepper. Place in a large, ovenproof sauté pan with the chicken stock and heat over medium heat just to a simmer.

Place the pan in the oven and poach the salmon until the flesh is opaque, but still medium rare, 12 to 15 minutes.

Transfer the fillets to a platter and cool to room temperature, or cover and refrigerate until ready to serve.

Serve with Provençal Mustard on the side.

Provençal Mustard

MAKES 1¾ CUPS

The French love their mustards, and they make them in a wide variety of flavors. One of our favorites is a red pepper and tarragon blend, which makes a perfect condiment for picnic food like the poached salmon or sliced filet of beef. Don't forget to try it spread on sandwiches, too!

2 large roasted red peppers, jarred, or homemade (page 96)

1 cup Dijon mustard

2 tablespoons white wine

1 tablespoon chopped fresh tarragon

1 tablespoon chopped fresh flat-leaf parsley

Freshly ground black pepper

Place the roasted peppers in a blender or food processor and process until smooth.

In a medium bowl, combine the roasted pepper purée, the mustard, wine, and herbs. Season with black pepper to taste.

Leftover Dividend: Salmon Salad

SERVES 2

Most of us forget what a great salad poached salmon can make, and this is a nice way to enjoy it for lunch or dinner the day after your picnic. The greens are mixed right into the salad for a more casual dish.

10 grape or cherry tomatoes

8 spears of cooked asparagus

1½ cups flaked poached salmon (2 fillets)

1 large bunch of arugula or watercress, stemmed

1 tablespoon chopped fresh flat-leaf parsley

½ teaspoon sea salt

Freshly ground black pepper

¼ cup Lemon Vinaigrette (page 31)

Halve the cherry tomatoes and place in a medium bowl. Cut the asparagus spears in ¼-inch pieces and add to the bowl with the salmon, greens, and parsley. Gently toss together. Season with salt and pepper. Add the vinaigrette and toss gently.

Breakfast

In a perfect world, breakfast would be that special hour in the morning when we calmly sit down to eat something healthy instead of the usual mad rush that it is. It's only during vacation and on quiet weekends that we have a chance to enjoy the leisure of that extra cup of coffee sipped on the deck while reading the newspaper. ◉ And, with just a little organization, even a simple breakfast can become special: Fresh fruit drizzled with a mint-infused syrup, toast topped with raspberry butter, and freshly baked lemon blueberry muffins are worlds better than the regular cereal routine and don't require a lot of extra effort. Just a bit more time in the kitchen can produce an impressive spread of puffy French toast with cherry maple syrup or an Alsatian frittata. ◉ When it comes to breakfast, it's a good idea to plan ahead. Muffins and scones can be made at home, frozen, and brought with you. Or purchase some store-bought bagels and muffins and top them with our easy-to-make fruit butters. That way, breakfast in bed—and that extra hour of sleep—can be a dream come true.

Simply Spectacular Scones

MAKES 8

Debra's former pastry chef at Aux Délices brought us this wonderful recipe. They are simply the best scones we've ever had. If you're not planning to spend vacation time baking, make a batch ahead of time, split each scone in half horizontally like an English muffin, and freeze them in plastic wrap. Then pop them in the toaster in the morning for a fresh-from-the-bakery breakfast treat.

⅓ cup plus 1 teaspoon sugar

3 cups all-purpose flour

2½ teaspoons baking soda

½ teaspoon cinnamon

6 ounces (1½ sticks) chilled unsalted butter, cut into cubes

1 cup finely chopped dried apricots (about 15)

¾ cup buttermilk

2 tablespoons heavy cream

Preheat the oven to 350 °F.

In a mixer with the paddle attachment, or by hand in a medium bowl, combine ¹/₃ cup of the sugar, the flour, baking soda, and cinnamon. Add the cubed butter and mix on slow speed until the mixture resembles coarse meal. Be careful not to over-mix; the batter should not come together at this point.

Stir in the apricots, then the buttermilk. Mix until the batter is moist, but not sticky.

Remove the dough from the bowl and roll out on a floured surface to a ³/₄-inch thickness. Cut into eight 3-inch rounds (an empty, clean can or glass makes a good dough cutter). Place the scones on a baking sheet, brush with the heavy cream, and sprinkle with the remaining teaspoon of sugar.

Bake for 25 minutes, rotating the pan 180 degrees after 10 minutes, until the scones are golden brown.

> **Tip:** The secret to light-textured scones is not to over-mix the dough at any stage of preparation. While apricots are great year-round, we like to substitute chopped crystallized ginger or dried currants and raisins during winter.

Raspberry Butter

MAKES 2 CUPS

Dress up weekend brunch or add a surprise to everyday breakfasts with this easy-to-make flavored butter, which is heavenly when spread on toast, muffins, and bagels. Make a whole pound at a time, because it freezes beautifully. Blackberries and strawberries work well, too.

1 pound unsalted butter, cubed and softened

½ pint raspberries

2 tablespoons confectioners' sugar

In a blender or food processor, purée the butter, berries and sugar until blended.

NOTE: If using a blender, pulse on medium and carefully press the butter mixture down with a spatula, turning the machine off occasionally and scraping the sides. If you don't have a blender or food processor, just chop the berries before mixing them in to the butter and sugar.

> **Tip:** Chill the butter slightly in the refrigerator for 10 minutes. Spoon the butter into small ramekins or shape it into logs, wrap in plastic wrap, and chill or freeze until ready to use.

Lemon Blueberry Muffins

MAKES ABOUT 16 REGULAR OR 12 SUPERSIZE MUFFINS

While this lemon-blueberry duo is our warm-weather muffin of choice, this recipe easily adapts to other fruit combinations like pear–crystalized ginger, raspberry, and peach. Try adding orange zest instead of lemon if it seems like a better match. We like to mix up an entire batch or two at the beginning of the week using disposable muffin tins. Then we freeze them in groups of four in plastic bags to enjoy every morning.

3 cups unsifted all-purpose flour

1 cup granulated sugar

4½ teaspoons baking powder

½ teaspoon sea salt

2 large eggs

½ cup canola oil

1½ cups milk

¼ teaspoon cinnamon

¼ cup grated lemon zest (from 2 large lemons)

1½ cups blueberries

Sugar in the Raw (optional)

Nonstick cooking spray or 2 tablespoons melted unsalted butter

Preheat the oven to 350°F.

In a medium bowl, mix together the flour, sugar, baking powder, and salt.

In a separate bowl, whisk the eggs together. Stir in the oil and the milk.

Add the wet ingredients to the dry ingredients and mix until combined. Stir in the cinnamon, lemon zest, and blueberries.

Lightly grease a muffin pan with nonstick spray or melted butter and fill each cup two-thirds full with the batter. Sprinkle the top of each muffin with Sugar in the Raw, if using.

Bake for 20 to 25 minutes, until a toothpick inserted in a muffin comes out clean.

Aunt Marion's Minted Fruit Salad

SERVES 6 TO 8

Geralyn's aunt Marion is an amazing gardener who keeps her supplied with bunches and bunches of fresh mint all summer. While it makes a beautiful garnish and adds a sweet, clean note to salads and soups, one of our favorite ways to use it is in a mint-infused syrup, drizzled over a bowl of freshly cut fruit. We think strawberries and blueberries are a must to include early in the summer, and we look forward to August for its white peaches and cherries, but use any combination of the best fruit you can find.

Combine all of the fruits in a large, colorful bowl. Drizzle the mint syrup on top and toss lightly to coat. Garnish with fresh mint.

½ medium cantaloupe, seeded and cut into 1-inch cubes

½ fresh pineapple, cut into 1-inch cubes (see tip, page 108)

1 nectarine, pitted and cut into 1-inch cubes

1 peach, pitted and cut into 1-inch cubes

6 strawberries, hulled and halved

3 fresh figs, quartered

Large handful of blueberries

4 tablespoons Mint Syrup (opposite)

Fresh mint, for garnish

> **Tip:** When cutting fruits with large pits, pick the ripest you can find. With a sharp knife, insert the tip until you feel the pit. Cut around the flesh in a circle. Twist the two halves in opposite directions and pull apart. The pit can now be easily removed.

Mint Syrup

MAKES 1¼ CUPS

Try using the syrup as a sweetener in iced tea or as a replacement for sugar in lemonade; the liquid sugar dissolves instantly in cold liquids and the mint adds a refreshing note to the drinks. We've also experimented with other herbs and found we enjoyed basil syrup drizzled over any kind of melon, and lavender syrup is another good choice with fruit salad. The syrups can be kept refrigerated for up to a week.

1 cup sugar

1 cup water

½ cup fresh mint leaves, coarsely chopped

In a small saucepan, bring the sugar and water to a boil over high heat. Reduce the heat to medium and let it boil for 3 to 4 minutes. Remove the pan from the heat and stir in the mint. When the syrup has cooled, transfer it to a container, cover, and place in the refrigerator. Allow the mixture to steep for at least 4 hours, but preferably overnight. Before serving, strain the mixture and discard the mint.

VARIATIONS

For basil syrup, substitute ¹/₂ cup of fresh basil leaves for the mint. For lavender syrup, use 1 tablespoon of dried lavender. Prepare the syrup as above.

Very Special French Toast

SERVES 4

Okay, these take a little extra effort, but we promise that they'll be worth it for a special breakfast. These toasts need to soak overnight so the thick slices sop up every bit of the egg mixture. If you can't prepare the bread the night before, use thinner slices and allow them to soak for about 2 hours, turning them over once. The final baking in the oven puffs them up almost like soufflés.

12 large eggs

1¾ cups milk

2 teaspoons vanilla extract

2 teaspoons cinnamon

1 teaspoon nutmeg

1¼-pound loaf of challah bread or dense white country bread

5 tablespoons unsalted butter

Cherry or blueberry maple syrup (page 81)

Preheat the oven to 350°F.

In a large bowl, whisk together the eggs, milk, vanilla, cinnamon, and nutmeg.

Slice the ends off the loaf, then cut into eight 1¹/₂-inch slices. Arrange the bread slices in a pan big enough to accommodate all of them in a single layer. Pour the egg mixture over the bread. Cover and refrigerate, preferably overnight, turning the bread slices once.

To serve, melt 2 tablespoons of the butter in a large sauté pan over medium heat until it starts to bubble. Add 3 of the soaked bread slices and cook until golden brown, about 3 minutes. Turn and cook for another 3 minutes, or until golden on both sides. Transfer the cooked toasts to a baking sheet. Brown the remaining bread slices in the same way, transferring them to the baking sheet when cooked.

Place the sheet of toasts in the oven and bake for 5 to 8 minutes, or until puffy.

Serve with cherry or blueberry maple syrup.

> **Tip:** Believe it or not, these freeze beautifully after they are cooked. Wrap each piece individually in plastic wrap and place in the freezer. After defrosting them, you can reheat them in a sauté pan or in the microwave.

My Kids' Favorite Banana Pancakes

MAKES EIGHTEEN 4-INCH PANCAKES

Whether at home or on vacation, pancakes are a family affair at Debra's house every Saturday morning, and banana is her children's favorite kind. But don't limit yourself: blueberries, strawberries, and nectarines all taste equally delicious. Try lightly toasting the pecans for a decidedly adult flavor, or substitute chopped walnuts. If you are a purist and prefer your pancakes plain, serve them with one of the flavored butters or syrups on page 73 and opposite.

2 large eggs

2 cups buttermilk

6 tablespoons (¾ stick) unsalted butter, melted

1½ cups all-purpose flour

¼ cup sugar

2 teaspoons baking soda

½ teaspoon sea salt

1 cup diced bananas (2 large)

½ cup finely chopped pecans

Nonstick cooking spray or 2 tablespoons unsalted butter

In a medium bowl, whisk together the eggs and buttermilk. Stir in the melted butter.

In a small bowl, mix the flour, sugar, baking soda, and salt together.

Add the dry ingredients to the wet ingredients, stirring until just combined—don't worry if there are a few lumps. Stir in the bananas and pecans.

Lightly grease a large sauté pan or griddle with the nonstick spray or butter. Heat the pan until hot and then spoon out 3 tablespoons of batter per pancake. Cook the pancakes until the tops look dull and a few of the bubbles pop, about 3 minutes. Turn the pancakes over and cook for another minute.

Transfer the cooked pancakes to an ovenproof dish and place in a warm oven until the entire batch is ready to be served.

> **Tip:** These pancakes freeze well and make an "instant" flavor-packed breakfast. Place the pancakes in groups of 3 in individual plastic freezer bags. Just reheat them in your toaster oven or microwave.

Cherry Maple Syrup

MAKES 1½ CUPS

Debra's kids, Remy, Cole, and Gray, just love it when she gives their maple syrup a fruity twist. In August she buys those sweet, tart cherries that we can pop in our mouths all day long like candy, and she always makes sure to save enough for their Saturday pancake breakfasts. Don't be afraid to double the recipe, as the syrup keeps well in the refrigerator for up to 2 weeks.

1 cup pitted cherries, cut in half (about 25)

1 cup maple syrup

1 tablespoon cherry or raspberry preserves (optional)

In a small saucepan over medium heat, cook the cherries, syrup, and preserves, if using, until the mixture comes to a boil. Reduce the heat to medium-low and simmer for about 5 minutes, or until the cherries are soft.

Serve warm or at room temperature.

VARIATION

Make blueberry syrup by substituting 1½ cups of blueberries and a tablespoon of blueberry preserves.

Alsatian Frittata

SERVES 6

Think of a frittata as a fluffy quiche without a crust—an easy one-dish meal that's great for impressing weekend guests. Even better, it tastes just as good served warm right out of the oven or cooled to room temperature, so it's perfect for those houses where some wake up early and others like to sleep in.

Preheat the oven to 350°F.

Grease an 8-inch ovenproof sauté pan with nonstick cooking spray or butter and heat over a medium flame until hot, but not smoking.

In a large bowl, whisk together the eggs, half-and-half, salt, and pepper. Pour the egg mixture into the hot pan and sprinkle on the cheese, ham, and parsley. Cook for 1 minute more, then place in the oven for 30 to 35 minutes, turning the pan 180 degrees halfway through baking. The frittata is done when it looks fluffy and the center is set.

Turn the frittata onto a serving plate or cutting board and cut into 6 wedges.

Nonstick cooking spray or 2 tablespoons unsalted butter

12 large eggs

1½ cups half-and-half

1 teaspoon salt

Freshly ground black pepper, to taste

1½ cups grated Gruyère cheese

1½ cups chopped Black Forest ham or other good-quality ham (about 8 thin slices)

1 tablespoon chopped fresh flat-leaf parsley

VARIATION: Mediterranean Vegetable Frittata

If you grill the vegetables when you prepare dinner the night before, this is easy to put together in the morning. You'll only need 2 cups of the grilled vegetables for this recipe, but the leftovers are great to use as a side dish or tossed into a pasta salad.

1 small zucchini, trimmed

1 small yellow squash, trimmed

1 Japanese eggplant (or a small eggplant)

1 medium red, yellow, or orange bell pepper, seeded

2 tablespoons olive oil

Sea salt and freshly ground black pepper, to taste

2 teaspoons fresh thyme leaves, chopped

Nonstick coating spray or 2 tablespoons unsalted butter

Cut each of the vegetables in half lengthwise and then into quarters to form long spears. Cut the pepper into 1-inch wide strips. Place all of the vegetables into a large bowl, add the oil, and toss to coat. Season the vegetables with salt and pepper.

On a medium-hot grill, roast the vegetables about 7 minutes, turning frequently, until tender. Chop the roasted vegetables into half-inch pieces. You should have about 3¹/₂ cups.

Finish making the frittata as above, substituting 2 cups of the grilled vegetables and the thyme for the ham, cheese, and parsley.

Honey Nut Granola

MAKES 7 CUPS

We've served this versatile treat for breakfast with milk and fresh fruit, packed it to go for a midafternoon snack, and sprinkled it over vanilla ice cream for a last-minute dessert. It stays nice and crunchy for up to 2 weeks when stored in a resealable plastic bag or a container with a tight lid.

½ cup honey

½ cup (packed) dark brown sugar

1½ teaspoons vanilla extract

2 cups oats

1 cup sunflower seeds

1 cup sliced or slivered almonds

1 cup sweetened shredded coconut

1 cup chopped walnuts

Nonstick cooking spray or 2 tablespoons unsalted butter

Preheat the oven to 325°F.

In a small saucepan, cook the honey, brown sugar, and vanilla over medium heat until the sugar melts, stirring occasionally.

In a medium bowl, combine the oats, sunflower seeds, almonds, coconut, and walnuts. Add the sugar mixture and toss until the granola is evenly coated.

Lightly grease a baking sheet with the spray or butter and spread out the mixture in an even layer. Bake for 25 minutes, stirring the mixture once or twice during baking. Remove the granola from the oven, and let it cool to room temperature in the pan. Break the granola into chunks and store in a plastic bag or container.

Get-Up-and-Go Yogurt Shake

SERVES 3 TO 4

Can't wait to start the day? This healthy shake is packed with flavor and vitamins. While this strawberry-mango version is pretty awesome, some other favorite combinations include blueberry, strawberry, and peach; raspberry, strawberry, and nectarine; and cherry all by itself. If you would like a slightly sweeter concoction, add a tablespoon of honey and blend again.

1 cup strawberries (about 5 medium to large), hulled and quartered

1 large mango, peeled and cut into 1-inch chunks (about 1 cup)

1 cup low-fat plain yogurt

1 cup ice

Place all of the ingredients in a blender. Purée until smooth. Serve icy cold.

From the Farm Stand

A ren't some of your best food memories about summer vegetables? Sliced beefsteak tomatoes so juicy that they're best eaten in your bathing suit. Waiting with an impatient appetite for peak corn season and then eating so many butter-slathered ears that you thought you would pop. Raw green beans so crunchy and sweet that you have to buy an extra pound because you can't stop snacking on them during the drive home.　　We were both lucky to grow up in New Jersey. Before green markets and prior to the era of fancy specialty foods stores, there were old-fashioned farms, like Delicious Orchards and Wightman's, where our moms bought our fruit and veggies every week and we went apple and pumpkin picking. We were lucky again because we both moved to New York City at just about the same time that urban green markets began to flourish, when farmers taught us concrete dwellers to appreciate the intense flavors of fruits and vegetables that had been picked just hours before we ate them.

Almost anywhere you travel these days, you can find a farm stand or a weekend green market that showcases the local best. And while a farm stand may not grow the exotic lettuce mix you find at your supermarket or stock tropical fruits, every one of them has bins upon bins of seasonal treasures, from zucchini, basil, and beans to strawberries, peaches, and cherries. We say buy them all, because when it comes to produce, you've got to go for the freshest you can find and build from there.

We are big advocates of allowing the flavor of each ingredient to stand on its own, and summer corn and tomatoes might not need more than a quick cooking or a touch of salt to become a delicious addition to any meal. But, as you will see, with just a little creativity and not too much fuss, their vibrant flavors can be transformed into soups and salads that will become the centerpiece of your meal.

Peppery Arugula and Potato Soup

SERVES 10 TO 12

Spicy arugula makes for a welcome warm-weather variation on classic potato soup. We like it served both warm and cold, but prefer it chilled in the summer. During the winter, try substituting watercress or fennel for the arugula for a tummy-warming adaptation.

In an 8-quart soup pot, melt the butter over medium heat. Add the leeks and onion and cook until softened, stirring occasionally, about 15 minutes. Add the potatoes and chicken stock and bring to a boil over high heat. Lower the heat to medium and simmer until the potatoes are tender, 15 to 20 minutes.

Add the cream and return the soup to a boil. Reduce the heat to medium and simmer for an additional 10 to 15 minutes. Stir in the arugula, salt, and pepper.

Working in batches, purée the soup in a blender or food processor until smooth. Taste the soup and reseason if necessary. Serve warm or chilled.

3 tablespoons unsalted butter

4 medium leeks (white part only), cleaned, halved lengthwise, and cut into ¼-inch half-moons

1 small onion, sliced

3 medium potatoes, peeled and diced

9 cups chicken stock or low-sodium canned chicken broth

1 cup heavy cream

2 large bunches of arugula

2½ teaspoons sea salt

8 generous grindings of black pepper

Jersey Corn Chowder

SERVES 8

Take it from two Jersey girls—there can never be too much Jersey corn, and there are never enough ways to eat it! Even diehard corn purists who raise an eyebrow at embellishing fresh corn with anything more than butter and salt will love this summertime chowder. It is very light and relies on ripe corn for its sweet, fresh flavor—in fact, you can omit the cream completely for an even lighter-bodied corn and vegetable soup. But don't forget the basil; it adds a delicate note that just sings summer.

In a large soup pot, melt the butter over low heat. Turn up the heat to medium-low and add the onions, carrots, and celery. Cook for 10 minutes, or until the vegetables have released their juices and have softened slightly.

Stir in the corn and the thyme. Add the stock, increase the heat to high, and bring to a boil. Reduce the heat to medium and allow the soup to simmer for 25 minutes. Add the potatoes and cream and cook for an additional 15 minutes, or until the potatoes are tender.

Remove the pot from the heat. Season with the salt and pepper, and stir in the herbs.

2 tablespoons unsalted butter

1 medium onion, diced

2 carrots, diced

3 celery stalks, diced

3¾ cups fresh corn kernels (5 medium ears; see tip, page 164)

2 teaspoons finely chopped fresh thyme leaves

8 cups chicken stock or low-sodium canned chicken broth

2 medium potatoes, peeled and diced

1 cup heavy cream

2½ teaspoons sea salt

Generous amount of freshly ground black pepper

2 teaspoons finely chopped fresh basil leaves

2 teaspoons finely chopped fresh tarragon leaves

Farmer's Market Zucchini Soup

SERVES 6 TO 8

Debra first made this soup at a farm-stand demonstration in her hometown of Greenwich, Connecticut. The idea was to pick anything on the farmer's stand that struck her fancy and then make a simple, impromptu dish. The abundance of beautiful green zucchini inspired this simple blender soup. It was such a hit that she began to offer it at her shop, where it has become an Aux Délices classic. Serve it chilled in the summer or warm, garnished with olive-oil croutons, in the cooler weather.

2 tablespoons unsalted butter

2 medium carrots, sliced

3 celery stalks, sliced

1 small onion, sliced

2 teaspoons chopped fresh thyme leaves

5 medium zucchini, trimmed, cut in half lengthwise, and sliced in ½-inch moons (about 7½ cups)

6 cups chicken stock or low-sodium canned chicken broth

2 teaspoons sea salt

In an 8-quart soup pot, melt the butter over medium heat. Add the carrots, celery, and onion and sauté for 10 minutes, stirring occasionally. Add the thyme, zucchini, and stock, increase the heat to high, and bring to a boil. Reduce the heat to medium and simmer for 10 minutes, or until the zucchini are tender. Stir in the salt.

Working in batches, purée the soup in a blender or food processor until smooth. Serve warm or chilled.

> **Tip:** For a quick, elegant first course for eight, sauté 8 large sea scallops until just done—about 2 minutes on each side. Place a sea scallop in the middle of each bowl of the chilled zucchini soup.

Chilled Sugar Snap Pea Soup

SERVES 8

We can hardly resist sneaking a few of these naturally sweet beans right off the farm stand and eating them raw, but they also make a delicious cold soup. Buy a few pounds at a time so that half can be served steamed or sautéed with dinner while the remainder simmers on the stove to be puréed and refrigerated for tomorrow's lunch or supper.

2 tablespoons unsalted butter

1 small onion, sliced

2 celery stalks, sliced

1 carrot, sliced

1½ pounds sugar snap peas, strings removed

6 cups chicken stock, or low-sodium canned chicken broth

2 teaspoons sea salt

6 generous grindings of black pepper

20 fresh mint leaves

In an 8-quart soup pot over medium heat, melt the butter. Add the onion, celery, and carrot and sauté until they are tender, stirring occasionally, 10 to 12 minutes. Add the sugar snap peas and the stock, bring the soup to a boil over high heat, then reduce the heat to medium and simmer until the peas are just tender, about 3 minutes. Add the salt and pepper and set aside to cool a bit.

Working in batches, purée the soup in a blender along with the mint leaves, until smooth. Stir and refrigerate for at least 4 hours. Before serving, recheck the seasoning and adjust if necessary.

> **Tip:** To check the seasoning of a soup that you will be serving chilled, chill a small quantity in a bowl in the refrigerator. When it has cooled completely, taste it and adjust the seasonings; the colder temperature usually requires more aggressive seasoning.

Saratoga Summer Vegetable Salad

SERVES 6

Crunchy and colorful, this country take on a Greek salad uses vegetables that can easily be found in your garden or even at the smallest local grocery. The crumbled Roquefort really dresses up this uncomplicated salad, or, for a less rich flavor, sprinkle fresh goat cheese on top.

Cut the ends off the zucchini and squash and cut each in half horizontally. Stand each half on its end and cut off the peel along with about $1/2$ inch of the flesh. Cut the peels into a small dice. Reserve the cores for another use in soup or stock.

In a medium bowl, gently toss the zucchini, squash, bell pepper, celery, tomato, avocado, basil, parsley, and lemon thyme. Drizzle in the vinaigrette and add the salt, pepper, and cheese and toss again until mixed.

1 medium zucchini

1 medium yellow squash

1 red, yellow, or orange bell pepper, seeded and finely diced

3 celery stalks, finely diced

1 large tomato, cored, seeded, and finely diced

1 medium avocado, peeled, pitted, and finely diced

10 fresh basil leaves, thinly sliced

¼ cup chopped fresh flat-leaf parsley

2 tablespoons chopped fresh lemon thyme (optional)

½ cup Champagne Vinaigrette (page 32) or Lemon Vinaigrette (page 31)

¾ teaspoon sea salt

Freshly ground black pepper, to taste

¾ cup crumbled Roquefort cheese

Balsamic-Marinated Red Onions

SERVES 4

A great accompaniment for any grilled meat, these sweet-sour onions can turn a simple burger or sandwich into something special. Grill the onions until just tender, but still firm enough to retain their shape. The onions can also be broiled or, in a pinch, sautéed on the stovetop over medium heat.

2 red onions, cut into
¼-inch-thick slices

¾ cup balsamic vinegar

2 tablespoons sugar

Grated zest of 1 orange

Juice of 1 orange

Sea salt and freshly ground
black pepper, to taste

In a medium nonreactive bowl, add the onion slices, vinegar, sugar, zest, and juice. Cover with plastic wrap and refrigerate for at least 3 hours.

On a medium-hot grill or under the broiler, cook the onions for 5 minutes on each side, or until they are tender but still hold their shape. Remove from the grill and season with salt and pepper. Serve warm or at room temperature.

Roasted Red Peppers

This recipe explains how to roast peppers under a broiler, but you can also cook them on the grill. Either way, keep a careful watch on the peppers so that they are charred on the outside but not overcooked. Note that yellow and orange peppers roast much faster than red ones.

Preheat the broiler for at least 5 minutes. Line a baking sheet with aluminum foil.

Arrange the peppers on the baking sheet and broil as close to the heating element as possible until the skin begins to bubble and brown, about 5 minutes. Turn the sheet pan 180 degrees and continue to roast until the skin is puffy and charred but the flesh is still firm, 3 to 5 minutes longer. With tongs, turn the peppers over and repeat until all sides are roasted.

Transfer the peppers to a heat-resistant bowl and cover them with plastic wrap, allowing the peppers to steam in their skins for about 15 minutes. Peel the charred skin from the peppers, then remove the stems and seeds.

The roasted peppers can be stored in plastic wrap or a tightly covered container in the refrigerator for 5 to 7 days.

Oven-Roasted Tomatoes

SERVES 4 TO 6

6 ripe plum tomatoes, cored and split in half lengthwise

Sea salt and freshly ground black pepper, to taste

1 teaspoon herbes de Provence

There are so many delicious things to do with roasted tomatoes that you'll want to double or even triple the recipe to ensure leftovers. When drizzled with olive oil and some slivers of basil they make a quick side dish, and they are always a welcome addition to any pasta. Once roasted, the tomatoes freeze well in resealable plastic bags; or top them with olive oil and store in the refrigerator in a glass jar— they'll keep for a few days. (Photograph on page 86)

Preheat the oven to 275°F.

Season the tomatoes with salt and pepper and place them cut side up on a baking sheet. Sprinkle the tomatoes with herbes de Provence. Roast the tomatoes for 3 hours, or until they are shriveled and most of the liquid is gone.

Let the tomatoes cool to room temperature, then transfer to a covered container and refrigerate until ready to serve.

Green Garden Vegetable Salad

SERVES 6

Cooking the veggies in this beautiful salad until just barely tender gives it extra character and plenty of crunchy texture. While this version is dressed with lemon vinaigrette, which adds a cool summery note, it can just as easily be tossed with extra-virgin olive oil or an herb-flavored oil.

Sea salt

½ pound haricots verts or string beans, ends trimmed

½ pound asparagus, peeled and woody ends cut off

½ pound sugar snap peas, ends trimmed

¼ cup Lemon Vinaigrette (page 31) or 3 tablespoons extra-virgin olive oil

Freshly ground black pepper, to taste

Prepare an ice-water bath (see tip, page 47).

Meanwhile, bring 4 quarts of salted water to a boil. When the water boils, blanch the haricots verts for 3 to 4 minutes, until just tender. Transfer immediately to the ice bath and allow them to cool for 2 minutes. Drain them immediately.

Repeat the procedure for the other vegetables, blanching the asparagus for 4 minutes and the sugar snap peas for 2 minutes, cooling both in the ice-water bath.

Cut 2 inches from the tops of the cooled asparagus and cut the tops in half lengthwise. Cut the spears into $1^{1}/_{2}$-inch pieces.

In a large bowl, combine the haricots verts, asparagus, and sugar snap peas. Just before serving, toss the vegetables with the vinaigrette and season with salt and pepper.

NOTE: If you'd rather microwave the vegetables than blanch them, place each vegetable in a separate microwave-safe dish and cover with plastic wrap or its lid. Microwave on high: green beans for $3^{1}/_{2}$ minutes; the asparagus for 4 minutes; the sugar snap peas for 3 minutes. Place the vegetables in an ice bath immediately, removing them as soon as they are cool.

Roasted Corn Tabbouleh

SERVES 8

Middle Eastern dishes, with their wonderfully refreshing, earthy flavors, make perfect warm-weather eating. This recipe is a great way to use any leftover roasted corn, which adds a nice nutty flavor to the salad. While Debra always takes the time to blanch and peel the tomatoes, the home cook Geralyn usually skips this step to have 5 more minutes in the sun.

1½ cups bulgur wheat

2 cups boiling water

1 large tomato, cored

1½ cups grilled corn kernels from 4 ears (see Note)

2 cups peeled, finely diced cucumber (about 1½ medium)

½ red onion, finely diced

½ cup finely chopped fresh flat-leaf parsley

1½ tablespoons finely chopped fresh mint leaves

1½ teaspoons sea salt

Freshly ground black pepper, to taste

½ cup extra-virgin olive oil

Juice of 1 large lemon

Place the bulgur in a large bowl. Pour the boiling water over the grain. Cover the bowl with plastic wrap and let the bulgur steep until it has absorbed all of the water.

Meanwhile, bring another small saucepan of water to a boil and make an ice-water bath (see tip, page 47).

Cut an X on the bottom of the tomato and place it in boiling water for 1 to 2 minutes, until the skin has loosened. Remove the tomato from the water and transfer it to the bowl of ice water. When the tomato has cooled, about 2 minutes, remove it immediately. Remove the skin, seeds, and ribs and cut the remaining flesh into a small dice.

Fluff the bulgur with a fork. Add the corn, cucumber, onion, tomato, parsley, and mint and mix together. Season with salt and pepper. Add the oil and lemon juice and toss until well combined.

NOTE: If you are not using leftover cooked or grilled corn, place the kernels on a sheet pan and roast them at 350°F. for 20 to 25 minutes, until soft.

French Country Potato Salad

SERVES 8 TO 10

Good old American potato salad is a great choice for burgers and dogs, but this rustic French-style salad is an elegant alternative that will dress up your menu. We find that steaming the potatoes makes a better-tasting salad; the potatoes don't break down in the water, so they look prettier, plus they taste less starchy.

3 pounds small creamer potatoes (about 30), unpeeled and scrubbed well

4 pieces leek (white part only), split lengthwise and thinly sliced

2 roasted red peppers, jarred or homemade (page 96)

2 tablespoons chopped fresh thyme leaves

2 teaspoons chopped fresh tarragon leaves

⅔ cup Champagne Vinaigrette (page 32)

2 tablespoons Dijon mustard

2 teaspoons sea salt

½ teaspoon freshly ground black pepper

In a pot with a steamer insert, steam the potatoes until tender, about 15 minutes. (The potatoes can also be cooked in boiling salted water for the same amount of time.) Remove from the heat and let cool to room temperature.

In a pot of boiling water, blanch the leeks for 30 seconds, or until tender. Rinse in cold water and drain. Set aside.

Cut the roasted peppers in half crosswise and then cut them into half-inch slices.

Cut each potato into 8 pieces. In a medium bowl, mix the potatoes, leeks, peppers, thyme, and tarragon. In a separate bowl, stir together the champagne vinaigrette with the mustard. Drizzle the vinaigrette on the potato salad and toss gently until the vinaigrette coats the salad evenly. Season with the salt and pepper and toss again.

From the Dock

When temperatures rise and appetites wane, our longing for lighter meals is usually best satisfied by fresh seafood. We just can't get enough of the bass, tuna, and cod that run in massive schools all summer long off the Atlantic shores. They make some of the healthiest, easiest, and most elegant dinners we know. ⬤ We find it practical (and delectable) to pair our catch with seasonal produce—cucumbers, plums, tomatoes, and watermelon—mixing and matching them in sometimes surprising ways to obtain a delightfully different combination of flavors. If you are lucky enough to be vacationing near the water, swing by that local fish place on your way home from the beach and see what surprises the day's catch brought in. We often cook an extra pound or so of tuna, shrimp, or crab because they taste so good at room temperature the next day. It's a snap to turn last night's dinner extras into a "dressed up" salad—the perfect choice for a special sit-down lunch or a casual supper on those really hot days.

Malibu Soft-Shell Crab Salad

SERVES 4

If the closest your summer house gets to the sound of waves crashing on the shore is an evening rental of Beach Blanket Bingo, *try this pretty salad with its tropical-colored slivers of orange and pink and its delicate crab flavor. Use the other half of the watermelon to make a batch of Watermelon Coolers (page 40) for you and Moon Doggie to sip beforehand.*

Cut the watermelon half lengthwise. Slice each quarter lengthwise again to create 4 wedges. Remove the flesh from the rinds and cut enough of the watermelon to have 16 1/4-inch-thick triangular slices.

Cut the fennel into very thin 1-inch-long slices. Cut the red onion slices in half to make half-moon–shaped slivers.

Rinse the arugula and dry it thoroughly with paper towels. In a large bowl, toss together the arugula, basil, red onion, lemon peel, and fennel. Add the lemon vinaigrette and toss until the arugula is evenly coated. Add the orange segments and watermelon and toss gently to mix, being careful not to break up the watermelon pieces. Season with salt and pepper.

Season the crabs with salt and pepper. In a medium sauté pan, heat 1 tablespoon of the oil to almost smoking. Place 4 crabs in the pan, and sauté them for 2 minutes on each side. Remove to paper towels. Repeat the process with the remaining oil and crabs.

To serve, place a quarter of the salad mixture on a plate. Top each with 2 soft-shell crabs and serve immediately.

½ small seedless watermelon

1 medium fennel, cored and fronds removed

½ medium red onion, thinly sliced

4 small bunches of arugula, stems trimmed

10 large basil leaves, sliced

2-inch piece of lemon peel, sliced into very thin strips

¼ cup Lemon Vinaigrette (page 31)

2 large oranges, cut into segments (see tip)

Sea salt and freshly ground black pepper, to taste

8 medium soft-shell crabs

2 tablespoons canola oil

> **Tip:** To make pretty orange segments, remove the peel with a sharp knife, making sure to cut away the pith and expose the orange flesh. Carefully cut on each side of the membrane and remove the flesh from each.

Grilled Swordfish with
Sweet and Sour Onion Relish

SERVES 4

We first cooked this after our families had spent a day splashing around in Deb's pool. It was an impromptu recipe, made with things we found when we opened the refrigerator. The tangy-sweet flavor and the great crunchy texture of this onion relish made it such a perfect companion to the swordfish that we retraced our steps and wrote down the recipe. (It works just as well with other meaty fish like tuna, mahimahi, and salmon.) To get the most intense flavor punch out of the relish, make it the night before so that all of the flavors can develop fully.

1 large carrot, cut into matchstick pieces

1 cup rice wine vinegar

4 tablespoons sugar

1 English seedless or regular cucumber, peeled, trimmed, and cut in matchstick pieces

1 large Vidalia onion, cut in half and thinly sliced

2 teaspoons crushed coriander seed (optional)

4 tablespoons chopped fresh cilantro leaves

4 swordfish steaks (5 ounces each)

Sea salt and freshly ground black pepper, to taste

4 teaspoons canola oil

In a small pot, bring water to a boil. Blanch the carrots for about 1 minute, until they have softened slightly but are still al dente. Drain and rinse with cold water.

Combine the rice wine vinegar and sugar in a small pan and simmer until the sugar is dissolved.

In a medium bowl, mix together the carrots, cucumber, and onions and pour the hot rice wine mixture over them. Stir in the coriander and the cilantro. Cover the onion relish with plastic wrap and refrigerate for at least 1 hour.

Prepare a hot grill.

When you are ready to serve, season the swordfish with salt and pepper and rub both sides of each steak with the oil. Grill the swordfish for 2 minutes, then turn and cook for 1 to 2 more minutes, or until the flesh is firm and opaque.

Serve with the relish spooned on top of the fish.

Cod with Oven-Roasted-Tomato Vinaigrette

SERVES 4

Sometimes, when you use just the right combination of raw ingredients, you create a dish that is so much better than the sum of its parts—and this cod dish is a perfect example. While its simplicity makes it right for the summer house state of mind, the meatiness of the cod and the hearty flavor of oven-roasted tomatoes makes it a favorite of ours even in the cooler weather.

4 cod fillets (6 ounces each)

Sea salt and freshly ground black pepper

¾ cup plus 2 tablespoons extra-virgin olive oil

1 teaspoon herbes de Provence

1 tablespoon chopped fresh tarragon leaves

1 tablespoon chopped fresh thyme leaves

¼ cup champagne vinegar

6 Oven-Roasted Tomatoes (page 97)

Preheat the oven to 450 °F.

Season the cod with salt and pepper. Heat 2 tablespoons of the oil in an ovenproof sauté pan until smoking. Place the fillets in the pan, skin side up, and sauté for 1 minute, or until the cod is seared. Place the pan in the middle of the oven and roast until the flesh is firm and opaque, 12 to 15 minutes, depending on the thickness of the fish.

Meanwhile, in a medium bowl whisk together the herbs, vinegar, and 1 teaspoon salt until the salt dissolves. Chop the roasted tomatoes into a large dice and add them to the bowl. Slowly whisk in the remaining ³/4 cup of oil and season with pepper.

To serve, spoon ¹/2 cup of the vinaigrette over each fillet.

Peppered Salmon with Pineapple Compote

SERVES 4

Almost everyone loves this meaty fish, but how do you transform plain-Jane grilled salmon into a remarkable dinner? Serve it with this refreshing, sweet and spicy compote, which combines fresh pineapple and honey with hot chipotle pepper for a flavor that brightens up every bite.

2 tablespoons unsalted butter

2 cups pineapple (half of a small one), cut into large chunks (see tip)

2 tablespoons honey

½ large canned chipotle chile in adobo

¾ cup orange juice

4 large mint leaves

2 teaspoons olive oil

4 salmon fillets (6 ounces each)

Sea salt and freshly ground black pepper, to taste

In a sauté pan over medium-high heat, melt 1 tablespoon of the butter. Add the pineapple and cook for about a minute. Stir in the honey and the chile and continue to cook, mixing occasionally, until the pineapple has caramelized, about 4 minutes. Reduce the heat to low, add the orange juice, and allow it to reduce by three quarters.

Place the pineapple mixture in a blender or food processor and add the mint. Purée until smooth. This should yield about 1 cup. Transfer the purée to a bowl, cover with plastic wrap, and cool in the refrigerator.

Prepare a hot grill.

Lightly oil the salmon with the olive oil and season with salt and pepper on both sides. Place the fish, skin side up, on the grill and cook for 2 minutes. Using tongs, turn the fillets 45 degrees to create a crosshatch pattern and grill for 2 more minutes. Turn the fillets over and continue to grill until the salmon is medium rare, about 3 more minutes, depending on the thickness of the fillet.

Serve the salmon crosshatch side up with the pineapple compote on the side.

> **Tip:** To prepare a pineapple, cut off the top and bottom, then stand the fruit up on a cutting board. Slice off the rind using even, downward strokes. Remove the core by cutting a half-moon slice vertically as close to the core as possible. Turn the pineapple a quarter turn and repeat until you have 4 long half-moon chunks, which can then be sliced as desired.

Sea Scallops with Summer Squash

SERVES 4

Who knew that everyday zucchini could be dressed up so easily by simply pairing it with succulent scallops? Better still, this casually elegant supper goes from stovetop to the table in less than 30 minutes.

5½ tablespoons unsalted butter

6 large shallots, peeled and thinly sliced

3 medium garlic cloves, thinly sliced

2 large zucchini, trimmed and thinly sliced in rounds

2 large yellow squash, trimmed and thinly sliced in rounds

Leaves from 8 sprigs of thyme

1½ cups chicken stock or low-sodium canned chicken broth

2 tablespoons canola oil

16 large sea scallops (about 1¾ pounds), cleaned

Sea salt and freshly ground black pepper, to taste

In a sauté pan, melt 4 tablespoons of the butter over medium heat. Add the shallots and garlic and sauté until translucent, about 2 minutes. Reduce the heat to low and add the zucchini, squash, and thyme, stirring occasionally. Sauté the vegetables until they are slightly caramelized, 5 to 7 minutes.

Add the chicken stock and simmer until it is reduced by half. Swirl the remaining 1½ tablespoons of butter into the vegetable mixture until it has emulsified into the stock. Remove the sauce from the heat.

Meanwhile, in a large sauté pan, heat the canola oil until hot. Season the scallops on both sides with salt and pepper and add to the pan. Cook on one side for about 1½ minutes or until golden brown, then turn and cook for 1½ minutes more until the scallops are just cooked through.

To serve, place 4 scallops on each plate and spoon the vegetables and sauce around them.

Sea Bright Striped Bass

SERVES 4

During a brief few weeks of summer every avid fisherman hopes that the day's catch will include some of the prized striped bass that run up and down the East Coast. Geralyn has fond memories of her neighbor Mr. Oswald beach-casting day after day off the beaches of tiny Sea Bright, New Jersey; but it wasn't until he finally gave her one of his catch to take home for dinner that she understood his passion for the fishing life. Of course, a quick trip to the fish market after a relaxing day at the beach is so much easier and the dish tastes just as sweet. . . .

1 large peach, pitted and quartered

1 large nectarine, pitted and quartered

1 large plum, pitted and quartered

5 tablespoons extra-virgin olive oil

3 tablespoons balsamic vinegar

4 striped bass fillets (5 ounces each) or other meaty fish such as grouper

2 to 3 tablespoons canola oil

Sea salt and freshly ground black pepper, to taste

Prepare a medium-hot grill.

In a medium bowl toss the fruits with two tablespoons of the olive oil. With tongs, transfer the fruit to an oiled grill, and cook over medium heat until slightly soft, about 5 minutes, turning the pieces of fruit regularly.

Cut the grilled fruit quarters lengthwise into $1/2$-inch-thick slices and return to the mixing bowl. Drizzle with the remaining 3 tablespoons of olive oil and the balsamic vinegar.

Brush the fish with the canola oil and season with salt and pepper. Place the bass on the hottest spot of the grill, flesh side down, for 5 to 6 minutes. Turn the fish over and cook an additional 5 to 6 minutes.

To serve, place a fillet on each plate and top with some of the fruit.

Tuna Niçoise Salad

SERVES 4

During those dog days of summer when a hot meal seems just too much, this salad hits just the right balance. Debra's tip for preparing a top-notch composed salad: Season each ingredient separately before arranging it on the plate.

4 slices of tuna, about 1 inch thick (4 ounces each)

Sea salt and freshly ground black pepper

1 pound haricots verts or green beans, trimmed

¼ cup Sherry Shallot Vinaigrette (page 32)

4 small purple Peruvian, tiny new, or creamer potatoes

4 eggs, hard boiled, peeled and quartered

20 grape or cherry tomatoes

16 Niçoise olives

Thyme or summer savory leaves, for garnish (optional)

Prepare a medium-hot grill.

Season the tuna with salt on both sides and grill until medium rare, about 2 minutes on each side. Allow the fish to cool to room temperature and cut each tuna piece on the bias into 6 slices.

Meanwhile, in a large pot of boiling salted water, blanch the beans until tender, 2 to 3 minutes. Drain the beans from the water and dunk them in a bowl of ice water. As soon as they are cool, about 2 minutes, remove the beans from the water and pat them dry with paper towels. In a small bowl, toss them with half of the vinaigrette and season to taste.

Steam or boil the potatoes for 15 minutes, or until tender. Let them cool to room temperature, then quarter them and season with salt and pepper.

Season the eggs with salt and pepper.

To serve, fan six slices of tuna on a large white plate. Place a quarter of the potatoes to the right of the tuna. Stack a fourth of the beans in a sheaf on top of the potatoes. Place one quartered egg next to that. Place a fourth of the tomatoes in front of the beans and the olives in back. Drizzle the tuna with the remaining vinaigrette.

Sprinkle with thyme or savory, if you like.

Gulf Shrimp Salad

SERVES 4

We love pairing fruit with fish in the summertime. Its cool sweetness is a pleasant change from the heavier seasonings and sauces served with seafood during the winter. This salad makes for a beautiful presentation and a satisfying dinner when you're not in the mood to spend much time at the stove.
(Photograph on page 102)

20 large shrimp, peeled and deveined

1 ripe Hass avocado

2 ruby grapefruits

½ mango, finely diced

2 tablespoons chopped fresh tarragon leaves

2 tablespoons chopped fresh cilantro leaves

½ cup Lemon Vinaigrette (page 31)

Sea salt and freshly ground black pepper, to taste

Juice of ½ lemon

4 cups mesclun greens

Prepare an ice-water bath (see tip, page 47).

In a large pot of boiling water, cook the shrimp just until the flesh is opaque, about 3 minutes. Drain the shrimp and place in the ice-water bath. When cool, immediately drain well and pat dry with paper towels.

Cut the avocado in half lengthwise and remove the pit. Use a sharp knife to score the avocado flesh into a small dice and then scoop it out with a spoon into a large bowl.

Cut off the ends of the grapefruits and place them on a cutting board, standing each on its flat side. Remove the peel with a knife, making sure to cut away all the pith, exposing the pink flesh. With a sharp knife, remove segments by carefully cutting on each side of the membrane. Place in the bowl with the avocado.

Add the shrimp, mango, tarragon, and cilantro to the bowl. Toss with ¼ cup of the lemon vinaigrette, season with salt, pepper, and the lemon juice, and toss again.

Toss the greens with the remaining ¼ cup of vinaigrette, add to the shrimp mixture, and gently toss together. Divide among four chilled plates and serve.

From the Grill

We don't know why, but when it's hot outside, just about everything tastes better when grilled. Even people who don't like to cook like to barbecue; it's fun, it's accessible, and it doesn't require a lot of prep or cleanup. Everyone looks forward to those few short months when they can crank up the fire and cook until they can't eat another hot dog, burger, or rib.   ⦿   But we think the real secret to creating the best meals off the grill lies in the marinating and seasoning that happens beforehand. We like to take 10 minutes the night before to begin marinating tomorrow's dinner. It allows the meat to fully tenderize and absorb every morsel of seasoning. It also spares you prep after a day spent outdoors; you can just come home and fire up the grill. Once you do have your grill going, take advantage of it. We love opening the fridge to find extra grilled eggplant, fennel, corn, and meat for tonight's dinner as well as tomorrow's lunch.

Ginger Lime–Marinated Flank Steak

SERVES 4

Juicy, tender, and inexpensive, flank steak tastes best when marinated and grilled. A quick five minutes of prep the night before or while your coffee is brewing in the morning and then the steak goes from refrigerator to table in less than 20 minutes when you are ready for dinner.

2 garlic cloves, sliced

1 cup canola oil

1½ cups Soy, Ginger, and Lime Marinade (page 30)

2 pounds flank steak

In a shallow dish, combine the garlic, oil and the marinade. Place the steak in the dish and turn to coat both sides of the meat. Spoon a few tablespoons of the marinade on top of the steak, cover the dish with plastic wrap, and refrigerate. Marinate the steak for at least 6 hours, turning the meat over once.

Prepare a medium-hot grill.

Grill the steak for 7 to 8 minutes on each side for medium rare.

Remove the flank steak from the grill and let it rest for 5 minutes. To serve, slice the steak on the bias into 1/4-inch-thick slices.

Leftover Dividend: Thai Beef Salad

SERVES 4

In a medium bowl, toss together the beef, garlic, oil, lime juice and zest, soy sauce, salt, and pepper.

Add the watercress, onion, and scallions and toss again. Taste and check for seasoning. Add salt and pepper if necessary.

Divide evenly among 4 plates.

2 cups (1¼ pounds) thinly sliced leftover flank steak or beef filet

2 teaspoons chopped garlic

½ cup extra-virgin olive oil

Grated zest and juice of 1 lime

2 tablespoons soy sauce

1 teaspoon sea salt

Pinch of freshly ground black pepper

1 bunch of watercress or arugula, stemmed

¼ red onion, thinly sliced

3 scallions (white and green parts), sliced

Grilled Lamb Chops with Olive Butter

SERVES 4

Succulent lamb chops charred on the grill are always a special treat—elegant but casual, since you have to pick up the chops with your fingers to get at the best parts next to the bone. Any leftover olive butter tastes great smeared on baked potatoes or sourdough bread.

½ cup (1 stick) unsalted butter, softened

12 kalamata olives, pitted

12 large green olives, pitted

1 teaspoon herbes de Provence

⅛ teaspoon cracked black pepper

8 lamb chops, 1½-inches thick (about 2 pounds total)

2 tablespoons canola oil

Sea salt and freshly ground black pepper, to taste

In a food processor or blender, combine the butter, olives, herbes de Provence, and cracked pepper, processing until well blended and smooth, scraping the bowl once. Transfer the olive butter to a small bowl, cover with plastic wrap, and chill until firm.

Prepare a hot grill.

Rub the chops on both sides with the oil and season with salt and pepper. Cook the lamb chops on a hot grill for 2 minutes on each side. Move the chops to a medium-hot spot and continue to grill for 3 more minutes for rare to medium rare.

Transfer the chops to a platter and let them rest for about 5 minutes. Serve with a teaspoon of the olive butter on top of each chop.

Bay Head Barbecued Chicken

SERVES 6 TO 8

The best barbecue is all about the sauce, and this version is a classic. If you aren't lucky enough to have the proverbial rib and chicken "shack" near you, this recipe will satisfy those overwhelming urges for barbecue. Debra's method finishes the chicken in the oven, which seals the flavor of the sauce into the meat. The barbecue sauce will keep in the refrigerator for about 2 weeks in a tightly covered plastic container.

BARBECUE SAUCE

2 tablespoons olive oil

1 onion, sliced

2 garlic cloves, thinly sliced

1 red bell pepper, seeded and thinly sliced

3 cups ketchup

¼ cup molasses

1 tablespoon red wine vinegar

8 chicken breast halves, bone in

Sea salt and freshly ground black pepper, to taste

In a medium nonreactive saucepan, heat the oil over medium heat. Add the sliced onion and garlic and simmer for 3 to 5 minutes, stirring occasionally, until the onions are translucent. Add the bell pepper and cook 8 to 10 minutes longer, or until soft. Add the ketchup, molasses, and 1 cup water and bring to a boil over high heat. Lower the heat and simmer for 30 minutes, uncovered. Stir in the vinegar and simmer for 2 more minutes. Let the sauce cool to room temperature and transfer it to a plastic container.

Preheat the oven to 375 °F.

Prepare a hot grill. Line a baking sheet with foil.

Season the chicken with salt and pepper. Place the breasts on the grill skin side down and grill for about 2 minutes; using tongs, turn the meat 45 degrees to create a crosshatch mark and grill for 2 more minutes. Turn the breasts over and grill 2 minutes longer. Transfer to the baking sheet, skin side up.

Brush on a generous amount of barbecue sauce and bake for 20 minutes, or until the flesh is opaque and cooked through.

Texas-Style Baby Back Ribs

SERVES 6 TO 8

When our foodie friend Patty moved from Connecticut to Texas, we hounded her to find us the best method for falling-off-the-bone ribs. The trick to making these succulent, finger-licking-good ribs is to braise them in the oven first. This takes a little time, but the result is worth every minute. The barbecue sauce is added right before the ribs are finished on the grill, which seals in the smoky flavor and creates a crunchy crust.

2 tablespoons canola oil

2 full racks baby back ribs (4½ pounds)

6 quarts chicken stock, low-sodium canned chicken broth, or water

3 cups barbecue sauce (opposite)

Sea salt and freshly ground black pepper, to taste

Preheat the oven to 375°F.

In a large sauté pan over a high flame, heat the oil until almost smoking. Add the ribs, flesh side down, and sear them for 2 to 3 minutes, until they have nice color.

Transfer the ribs to a roasting pan large enough to accommodate all of them in one layer. Add the stock and cover the pan with aluminum foil. Place the roasting pan in the oven and cook for 3 to 3½ hours, or until fork-tender.

Remove the ribs from the oven and allow them to cool in their own liquid. At this point, you can keep them overnight in the refrigerator before finishing them.

Prepare a medium-hot grill.

Brush the ribs with barbecue sauce and season with salt and pepper. Place the ribs flesh-side down on the grill. Cook, turning once, for 6 to 8 minutes, basting the ribs with sauce, until the sauce has formed a crispy crust.

> **Tip:** If you'd prefer to finish the ribs in the oven rather than on the grill, preheat the oven to 475°F. Transfer the ribs to a baking sheet, and bake for 15 to 20 minutes, turning once, until the sauce is baked on.

Cumin-Spiced Tuna
with Carrot Ginger Vinaigrette

SERVES 4

We love this combination of earthy, refreshing flavors paired with simply grilled tuna. Any extra carrot ginger vinaigrette tastes great tossed with greens—and if you add some leftover tuna, sliced scallions, and cucumber it makes for a delicious Asian twist on salade niçoise.

In a blender or food processor, process the carrots until fine. Add the fresh and pickled gingers and process again until fine, scraping the bowl as necessary. Add the vinegar and oil and process until smooth. For a slightly thinner vinaigrette, drizzle in a few more drops of vinegar.

Season the tuna with the fish rub and salt and pepper on both sides of the steaks. Prepare a medium-hot grill.

Cook the tuna for 2 to 3 minutes. With tongs, turn the fish over and grill for 2 to 3 minutes longer, or until medium rare. To serve, spoon some of the carrot ginger vinaigrette over each tuna steak.

3 large carrots, trimmed, peeled, and cut into medium dice

2 tablespoons ginger, peeled and sliced

2 ounces pickled ginger (optional)

4 tablespoons rice wine vinegar

¼ cup Ginger Oil (page 27) or canola oil

4 5- to 6-ounce tuna steaks

½ portion Herb Blend for Fish (page 28)

Sea salt and freshly ground black pepper

Summer Savory Filet Mignon with Roquefort Mustard

SERVES 4

The hot flames of the grill sear a filet of beef beautifully, keeping all those juices inside for tender, moist meat. The trick to perfect doneness is being patient and using a medium-low grill so that the outside doesn't burn. Serve it with the rich Roquefort mustard for a decadent dinner.

⅓ cup canola oil

3 shallots, thinly sliced

2 garlic cloves, thinly sliced

3 sprigs of summer savory or rosemary

1½ pounds filet mignon, cleaned and trimmed

1 cup Dijon mustard

¾ cup blue cheese, crumbled

In a shallow dish, combine the oil, shallots, garlic, and summer savory. Add the filet, turning once to coat all sides with the marinade. Marinate in the refrigerator for at least 12 hours, but preferably overnight, turning the meat one more time.

In a medium bowl, whisk the mustard and cheese together until smooth. For an even smoother sauce, use a blender, scraping the sides once or twice to fully combine the ingredients. Cover with plastic wrap and store in the refrigerator until ready to serve.

Prepare a medium-hot grill.

Sear one side of the filet for about 3 minutes. Using tongs, turn the meat and sear the other side. Move the meat to the coolest spot on the grill, turning it on all sides frequently, for 15 minutes or until medium rare.

Remove the meat from the grill and allow it to rest for 5 to 10 minutes. Slice and serve with the Roquefort mustard on the side.

Leftover Dividend: Rosemary Beef Salad

SERVES 4

While there is nothing as tasty as a filet of beef sandwich with some mayo and horseradish, we wanted a second option that is a little fancier way to serve leftover flank steak or filet.

In a medium bowl, combine all of the ingredients. Toss gently until the rosemary oil evenly coats the salad. Check the seasoning and adjust if necessary.

VARIATION
This salad can also be served as a sandwich in pita bread

2 cups (1¼ pounds) leftover filet of beef or flank steak

1 bunch of arugula or watercress, stems removed

½ large red or green bell pepper, seeded and sliced into thin strips

10 grape or cherry tomatoes, halved

2 tablespoons Rosemary Oil (page 25)

Sea salt and freshly ground black pepper, to taste

Curried Lobster Tails

SERVES 4

The very first thing Debra's grandpa Al always did when they arrived at their summer house on Cape Cod was to buy a dozen lobsters for their first night of vacation. Boiled lobsters are still a great vacation tradition, but we think these grilled curried tails are an amazing alternative that don't require so much effort to eat. The natural juices steam the tail meat in their shells, giving it a tender texture, and the curry adds a subtle earthy flavor to the sweetness of the lobster. This recipe only uses the tails of lobsters, but it would be a shame not to buy them whole and use the claw and body meat to make our decadent Bar Harbor Lobster Cakes (page 52) or your favorite recipe for lobster salad.

⅓ cup Lemon-Thyme Blend (page 28)

1 teaspoon curry powder

Juice of ½ lemon

4 lobster tails (5 to 6 ounces each)

In a medium bowl, stir together the lemon-thyme blend, curry, and lemon juice.

Using a sharp knife, cut through the lobster shell to split the tails lengthwise. Place them in a large bowl, pour the curry marinade on top, and gently toss until the tails are coated. Cover the bowl with plastic, refrigerate, and let the lobster marinate for at least 6 hours or overnight.

Prepare a medium-hot grill.

Cook the tails flesh side down for about 4 minutes. Turn them over and grill for 3 minutes, or until tender. Be sure not to turn the tails over again as you will lose the tasty juices that keep the lobster meat moist.

Transfer the lobster tails to a platter and serve.

VARIATION

For sweet, herb-flavored lobster, marinate the tails in the Lemon-Thyme Blend, omitting the curry and lemon juice. When the tails are turned flesh side up on the grill, brush a tablespoon of softened herbed butter on each tail.

Grilled Corn in the Husk with Flavored Butters

SERVES 6 TO 12

Always make more corn than you can eat at a sitting and use the leftovers as great additions to tossed salads or in side dishes like Roasted Corn Tabbouleh (page 100). The flavored butters are a creative shortcut that adds rich flavor to the grilled corn, and are a savory addition when melted over vegetables or grilled meat. Freeze the butters until ready to use.

12 ears of your favorite corn, as fresh as possible

Flavored butters (recipes follow)

Salt and freshly ground black pepper

Prepare a medium-hot grill. Peel the husks down the cobs without removing them. Pull off the silk and replace the husks. Place the corn on the grill and cook for a total of 10 to 12 minutes or until tender, turning the ears every few minutes.

Serve with flavored butters, or just with salt and pepper.

ROASTED PEPPER AND THYME BUTTER

Great on steamed or grilled corn, this red pepper and thyme butter is also wonderful on corn muffins and warm bread.

1 cup (2 sticks) unsalted butter, softened

2 shallots, peeled and finely chopped

2 roasted red bell peppers, jarred or homemade (page 96)

1 tablespoon chopped fresh thyme leaves

Sea salt and freshly ground black pepper

In a food processor or blender, blend the butter, shallots, roasted pepper, and thyme until smooth. Season with salt and pepper to taste.

Scrape from the bowl onto a sheet of plastic wrap and shape into logs or pack into ramekins and chill.

CHIPOTLE BUTTER

The hot chile has a smoky, sweet, almost chocolatey flavor that is outstanding with grilled corn.

1 cup (2 sticks) unsalted butter, softened

1 large canned chipotle pepper in adobo

In a food processor or blender, blend the butter and chile until smooth. Scrape from the bowl onto a sheet of plastic wrap and shape into logs or pack into ramekins and chill.

Grilled Moroccan Eggplant

SERVES 4 TO 6

This has long been a favorite that we enjoy every summer at Debra and Greg's annual barbecue. We use it the next day as a topping for chicken or lamb sandwiches, or with oven-roasted tomatoes and black olives for a tasty side dish. Roasted garlic makes a big difference here.

1 medium eggplant (about 1 pound)

½ cup extra-virgin olive oil, plus more for brushing the eggplant

Sea salt and freshly ground black pepper

3 cloves Roasted Garlic (page 19) mashed, or 1 garlic glove, very finely chopped

½ teaspoon ground cumin

Juice of 1 lemon

1 tablespoon coarsely chopped fresh cilantro, plus ¼ cup whole cilantro leaves for garnish

2 tablespoons chopped fresh flat-leaf parsley

Prepare a medium-hot grill.

Slice the eggplant into ¹/₂-inch-thick rounds. Brush the slices with olive oil on both sides and season with salt and pepper.

In a small bowl, combine the ¹/₂ cup of oil, ¹/₂ teaspoon salt and 2 grinds of pepper, the garlic, cumin, lemon juice, chopped cilantro, and parsley.

Grill the eggplant rounds for 3 to 4 minutes on each side, until soft but still holding their shape.

Transfer the eggplant from the grill to a platter and spoon the herbed oil mixture over the slices. Garnish with cilantro leaves. Serve warm or at room temperature.

Rainy Day Dinners

Sweatshirt weather is what we used to call those rainy days at the beach. While we kids whiled away hours playing board games, gin rummy, and hearts, our moms reveled in the cool fresh air that blew through the house and invited them to turn on their stoves and cook. ⊙ There's nothing like a chilly wind to revive your appetite after days of blistering heat and dinners of chilled soups and salads. Suddenly there's a craving for comforting foods that have been braised or roasted and an urge to fill your house with smells of all-day cooking. Make a pie from the bowl of peaches on your counter, stock up on some breakfast scones to last the next few days, and prepare a soul-warming stew or pork roast for dinner. ⊙ Our rainy day dinners can be made any season. A crisp roasted chicken and a stuffed leg of lamb, or a vegetable cassoulet just waiting for some crusty bread to sop up all the juices? That's worth a few raindrops any time.

Caramelized Onion–Spinach Dip

MAKES 2¼ CUPS

Remember how much everyone loved Lipton Onion Soup dip when you served it at parties? Well this updated, fresh version gets an even richer flavor from the caramelized onions, plus a healthy lightening up with the addition of spinach. Surround a bowl of this with bite-size pieces of your favorite raw vegetables for a guaranteed crowd-pleaser.

- 1 tablespoon extra-virgin olive oil
- 1 medium onion, diced
- 1 garlic clove, chopped
- 8 ounces cream cheese, at room temperature
- ½ cup Crème Fraîche (page 22) or sour cream
- ½ cup (packed) cleaned and stemmed fresh spinach

In a medium pan heat the oil over medium heat. Sauté the onion and garlic until they are a deep golden brown, stirring occasionally, 4 to 5 minutes. Transfer to a bowl and let them cool slightly.

In a blender or food processor, combine the onion-garlic mixture, cream cheese, crème fraîche, and spinach and process until smooth, scraping the bowl at least once.

Season the dip with salt and pepper and transfer to a medium bowl. Cover with plastic wrap and place in the refrigerator until the dip has chilled and thickened slightly, about 30 minutes. Taste and adjust the seasoning if necessary.

Hearty Lentil Soup

SERVES 12

This lentil soup warms the belly whether it's a rainy summer day or a snowy winter one, and the leftovers taste even better, since the flavors have had a chance to combine and the soup thickens up. Make sure to use good-quality chicken stock or canned broth when preparing the soup as it is adds most of the flavor to the dish.

In a large soup pot, heat the oil and add the onion and garlic. Cook until the onions are soft, 3 to 4 minutes, stirring a few times. Stir in the carrots and celery and cook for 2 more minutes.

Add the lentils, chicken stock, thyme, and marjoram and bring the mixture to a boil over medium-high heat. Reduce the heat to medium and simmer for 40 to 45 minutes, until the lentils are tender. Season with salt and pepper.

2 tablespoons canola oil

1 large onion, diced

5 garlic cloves, sliced

1½ cups diced carrots (2 large)

1½ cups diced celery (3 ribs)

I pound lentils

10 cups chicken or vegetable stock, or low-sodium canned broth

2 tablespoons fresh thyme leaves, chopped

2 tablespoons fresh marjoram leaves, chopped

1 tablespoon plus 1 teaspoon sea salt

Freshly ground black pepper, to taste

Roasted Whole Red Snapper

SERVES 4

Spending the day at home with board games and cards can really work up a good appetite. And a big beautiful snapper that's just been pulled out of the ocean and roasted to perfection makes for some great eating. All it takes to prepare is a sprinkling of herbs, a squeeze of lemon, and—voilà, dinner is served. We've included a quick recipe for braised fennel, because we always seem to serve the two together. Be sure to get the fishmonger to scale and clean the fish for you.

1 2- to 2½-pound red snapper, scaled, gutted, and gills removed

Sea salt and freshly ground black pepper

Small bunch of fresh rosemary

Small bunch of fresh thyme

Small bunch of fresh tarragon

3 lemon slices

2 teaspoons olive oil

BRAISED FENNEL (optional)

2 tablespoons unsalted butter

2 large fennel bulbs, thinly sliced

2 cups chicken stock or low-sodium canned broth

Preheat the oven to 375°F.

With a sharp knife, make the opening in the fish cavity large enough to easily stuff with the herbs. Cut crosshatch marks about ¹/8 inch deep on both sides of the fish.

Season the cavity with salt and pepper and stuff it with the herbs and lemon. Drizzle 1 teaspoon of the olive oil in the cavity and rub the other teaspoon of oil on the skin. Season the ourside of the fish with salt and pepper.

Transfer the snapper to a lightly oiled baking sheet.

Place the fish in the oven and roast for 25 to 30 minutes, until the flesh is firm and opaque.

Meanwhile, in a large sauté pan over medium heat, melt the butter and sauté the fennel until it is slightly tender and has turned golden brown, about 10 minutes. Reduce the heat to low and add the stock. Cook for an additional 25 minutes, or until the fennel is soft and the stock has evaporated. Season with salt and pepper.

To serve, transfer the fish to a large platter and garnish with the braised fennel.

Crispy Roasted Chicken with Garlic and Herbs

SERVES 4

They say you can always tell a good cook by his roasted chicken. Well, we think this is a pretty foolproof recipe that doesn't require the more labor-intensive process of flipping the bird during the roasting. For the absolute tastiest results, start with the best-quality organic chicken you can find. We always roast a second bird to make chicken salad for a wonderful next-day lunch. (Photograph on page 130)

1 3½-pound chicken

Sea salt and freshly ground black pepper

10 sprigs of fresh thyme

2 sprigs of fresh tarragon

2 sprigs of fresh rosemary

4 large garlic cloves, sliced

2 tablespoons olive oil

Preheat the oven to 400°F.

Rinse the chicken well and pat dry. Season the cavity of the chicken generously with salt and pepper. Stuff the cavity with 4 sprigs of the thyme, the tarragon, and the rosemary. Place the slivers of garlic and the remaining thyme under the skin of the breast. Season the outside of the chicken with salt and pepper and drizzle with the oil.

Place the chicken in a roasting pan on the center rack of the oven. Roast for 1 hour, or until the skin is golden brown and the juices run clear when the leg is pierced with a fork. Remove from the pan and let the chicken rest 10 minutes before carving.

Leftover Dividend: Tarragon Tree Chicken Salad

SERVES 4

While roast chicken makes perfect rainy day fare, to us it's equally as delicious served at room temperature on a balmy evening. We immediately turn any leftovers into this salad, which Debra adapted from a pheasant salad she created at the Tarragon Tree, in Chatham, New Jersey. If you're not up to roasting, a supermarket rotisserie bird can stand in.

3 cups cooked chicken chunks (from 3½-pound chicken)

2 sprigs of tarragon, chopped

3 sprigs fresh thyme, chopped

4 fresh mint leaves, chopped

½ pint pear or cherry tomatoes, halved

4 thin slices red onion

⅓ cup Champagne Vinaigrette (page 32)

Combine all of the ingredients in a medium bowl, tossing until the vinaigrette coats the salad evenly.

Leftover Dividend: Early Harvest Chicken Salad

SERVES 4 TO 6

When the skies turn deep cornflower blue and the first pears appear at the green market, you know that autumn is just around the bend. This "transitional-season" salad takes advantage of late summer's bounty. In the colder months try substituting frisée or endive for the arugula, and turkey for the chicken—a delicious leftover idea for the holiday bird!

3 cups cooked chicken chunks (from 3½-pound chicken)

1 ripe pear, thinly sliced

2 small bunches of arugula

¼ cup chopped flat-leaf parsley

1 cup toasted walnut pieces

1 lemon

⅓ cup Lemon Vinaigrette (page 31)

1 teaspoon sea salt

Freshly ground black pepper

¾ cup crumbled Roquefort

In a medium bowl, toss together the chicken, pear slices, arugula, parsley, and walnuts. Using the large holes of your grater, remove the zest from the lemon and add to the bowl. Add the lemon vinaigrette and toss again until the dressing evenly coats the salad. Season with the salt and pepper. For a richer flavor, add the crumbled blue cheese.

Lobster, Mushroom, and Sweet Pea Risotto

SERVES 4

This easy-as-stirring recipe will dispel all fears you may ever have had of making risotto. Once you learn the basic recipe, you can flavor your risotto with anything that appeals to you. This is Debra's all-time favorite combination, but you can substitute any shellfish for the lobster, and Geralyn likes substituting a cup or two of white wine for some of the stock.

In a medium saucepan, bring the stock to a boil, then reduce the heat until the liquid is barely simmering.

In a heavy, large saucepan, melt the butter over medium heat. Add the onion and sauté for 4 to 5 minutes, until it is almost translucent. Stir in the Arborio rice until it is coated with the butter-onion mixture, then stir in the mushrooms.

Reduce the heat to medium-low. Ladle in $1/2$ cup of the stock and stir until it is almost completely absorbed by the rice. Continue to add the stock $1/2$ cup at a time, stirring frequently (it is not necessary to stir continuously) until each addition of the stock is absorbed into the rice before adding the next. Cook until the rice is tender but still al dente, about 30 minutes.

Stir in the cheese, then add the peas and lobster, cooking until the lobster is warm, 3 to 4 minutes. Season with the salt and pepper.

5½ cups chicken or vegetable stock, or canned low-sodium broth

2 tablespoons unsalted butter

1 medium onion, diced

1½ cups Arborio rice

6 ounces assorted wild mushrooms, stems removed if necessary, thinly sliced

¼ cup grated Parmigiano-Reggiano

1½ cups blanched fresh peas or good-quality frozen peas, defrosted

1½ pounds cooked lobster meat, cut into medium chunks (see opposite page)

1 teaspoon sea salt

Freshly ground black pepper, to taste

REMOVING THE MEAT FROM LOBSTERS

A 1¼-pound lobster yields about 4 ounces of meat from the tail and claws.

- To easily remove the meat from a lobster tail, cut down the "belly" with a sharp knife. Grasp the tail in both hands and split the shell vertically. The tail meat will come out in one piece.

- Remove the claws from the body with a firm twist, then separate the knuckles from the claws. Wrap the claw in a kitchen towel. With the blunt edge of a heavy knife, hit the claw in the middle and on either end. Unwrap and crack the shell. The claw meat should be able to be pulled out in one piece.

- To remove the meat from the knuckles, crack just below the joint with a knife, break it open with your fingers, and remove the meat.

Summer Vegetable Cassoulet

SERVES 4 TO 5

This soul-satisfying cassoulet is gratifying year-round, and can be served as a main course with salad and crusty bread or as a side dish topped with bread crumbs and butter and browned under the broiler until golden. In the winter months, we like substituting lima beans, peas, and butternut squash for the summer-only veggies. Allow enough time for this dish to rest before serving it so that every spoonful of broth can be absorbed into the vegetables.

2 tablespoons unsalted butter

1 medium onion, diced

4 garlic cloves, sliced

1 cup dried white beans, such as Great Northern

3¾ cups chicken stock or low-sodium canned broth

2 leeks (white part only), split lengthwise and thinly sliced

1 carrot, diced

½ medium eggplant, diced

½ large zucchini, diced

⅓ pound wax beans, trimmed

1½ tomatoes, quartered, cored, seeded, and sliced

2 teaspoons fresh thyme leaves

2¾ teaspoons sea salt

Freshly ground black pepper, to taste

In a deep-sided sauté pan or Dutch oven, melt the butter over medium-low heat. Add the onions and garlic and sauté until soft, about 5 minutes. Add the dried beans and 3 cups of the stock and increase the heat to medium-high.

Bring the mixture to a boil and then reduce the heat to medium-low. Add the leeks and carrots and simmer until the beans are almost tender, about 40 minutes.

Add the remaining ³/₄ cup of stock, the eggplant, zucchini, wax beans, tomatoes, and thyme. Raise the heat and bring the mixture to a boil again, cover the pot, and simmer for 10 minutes. Remove from the heat and season with the salt and pepper. The cassoulet should still be a little soupy at this point.

Turn on the broiler.

Mix together the bread crumbs, butter, herbs, salt, and pepper, and sprinkle on top of the cassoulet. Place under the broiler for 2 to 3 minutes, until the topping is golden brown.

BREAD-CRUMB TOPPING

1½ cups fresh bread crumbs

3 tablespoons melted unsalted butter

1 teaspoon herbes de Provence

¼ teaspoon salt

Freshly ground black pepper, to taste

Shrimp and White Bean Stew

MAKES 2 TO 3 MAIN-COURSE OR 4 APPETIZER SERVINGS

This is our ideal for the one-pot-comfort-food meal. Break out the Monopoly board while this simmers on your stove, and by the time you own Park Place, dinner will be ready.

Melt the butter in a large soup pot over medium-high heat. Add the leeks and sauté until soft, about 5 minutes. Add the beans, stock, and 2 tablespoons of the thyme and bring to a boil over high heat.

Reduce the heat to medium and simmer until the beans are al dente and most of the liquid is absorbed, 40 to 45 minutes. Add the tomatoes and continue to simmer over low heat until the beans are tender and there is a small amount of liquid remaining, about 10 more minutes.

Heat the oil in a sauté pan over medium-high heat. Add the shrimp and sauté until done, $1^1/2$ to 2 minutes on each side. Stir the shrimp into the stew.

Season with the salt and pepper. Just before serving, stir in the parsley and the remaining tablespoon of thyme.

2 tablespoons unsalted butter

3 large leeks (white part only), split lengthwise and sliced into 1-inch pieces

½ pound dried white beans (such as Great Northern or cannellini)

6½ cups chicken stock or low-sodium canned broth

3 tablespoons chopped fresh thyme leaves

24 grape or cherry tomatoes, halved

1 tablespoon canola oil

12 large shrimp, peeled and deveined

2 teaspoons sea salt

Freshly ground black pepper, to taste

2 tablespoons chopped fresh flat-leaf parsley

Sweet Corn Pudding

SERVES 8

Great for entertaining, this creamy, warm pudding is the next best thing to fresh corn on the cob. It's especially nice to serve at Thanksgiving if an Indian summer crop of good corn is still available; if not, use the best-quality frozen corn you can find, or better still, freeze your own at the end of corn season. To do so, simply remove the kernels from the cobs (page 164), portion them in resealable plastic bags, freeze, and enjoy all winter long.

4 cups corn kernels (from 6 to 7 medium ears)

6 eggs

1 cup heavy cream

1 cup milk

2 tablespoons fresh thyme leaves

½ cup all-purpose flour

1¼ teaspoons sea salt

¼ teaspoon freshly ground black pepper

1 tablespoon unsalted butter, for buttering the baking dish

Preheat the oven to 350°F.

Place 2 cups of the corn in a blender. Add the eggs, cream, milk, thyme, flour, salt, and pepper and cover the top with a towel. Pulse a few times and then process on low until the mixture is smooth.

Lightly butter a 6-cup baking dish. Pour in the corn mixture and then stir in the remaining 2 cups of corn. Place the baking dish in a larger roasting dish and place it in the oven. Pour hot water in the outer pan until it reaches halfway up the dish.

Bake the pudding for 1 hour, rotating the pan 180 degrees once during cooking. The pudding is done when the center is firm and the top is golden brown.

Tuscan Stuffed Leg of Lamb

SERVES 6 TO 8

Why bother getting any more complicated when simple tastes this good? A plain leg of lamb becomes an inspired meal when it's stuffed with goat cheese flecked with fresh parsley, garlic, and sun-dried tomatoes. The leftovers are definitely an added plus for yummy sandwich possibilities (see page 61).

- 1 tablespoon extra-virgin olive oil
- 2 tablespoons garlic, minced
- 8 ounces goat cheese
- ½ cup sun-dried tomato halves, softened and coarsely chopped (see Note)
- 1 cup (packed) coarsely chopped flat-leaf parsley
- 5-pound leg of lamb, cleaned, boned, and butterflied
- Sea salt and freshly ground black pepper, to taste
- 2 tablespoons fresh rosemary leaves, coarsely chopped (optional)

Preheat the oven to 425°F.

In a small sauté pan, heat the olive oil over medium-high heat and sauté the garlic until it is a light golden brown. Remove from the heat.

In a medium bowl, stir together the goat cheese, sun-dried tomatoes, garlic, and parsley.

Lay the butterflied lamb on a cutting board and season it with salt and pepper. If the meat is thicker in some areas, use a meat-tenderizing mallet and pound it until it is the same thickness throughout. Spread the goat cheese mixture in an even layer on the lamb, leaving a ½-inch border on all sides.

Cut six 12-inch lengths of kitchen string. Carefully roll the lamb jelly-roll style. Secure the rolled meat with string every 2 inches. Season the outside of the meat with salt and pepper and sprinkle with the chopped rosemary.

Place the lamb in a roasting pan in the middle of the oven for 1 hour, or until the internal temperature reaches 110°F. for medium rare. Remove the meat from the oven and allow it to rest for 10 to 15 minutes before slicing.

NOTE: To soften the sun-dried tomatoes, place them in a small bowl and cover with boiling water. Soak until soft, about 5 minutes. If you use sun-dried tomatoes packed in oil, skip the soaking step.

All-Afternoon Braised Breast of Veal

SERVES 6

This inexpensive cut of veal becomes fork-tender when it's slowly braised. We like to change the stuffing to fit the time of year—another favorite is sautéed spinach and mushrooms, with some sweet sausage added to the mix in the colder months.

Preheat the oven to 350°F.

In a large sauté pan, melt the butter over medium heat, then add the diced onions and sauté until tender. Add the Swiss chard and cook until tender, about 5 minutes. Remove from the heat and season with salt and pepper.

Make a shallow pocket in the veal by slicing from the large end to the pointed end, being careful not to slice through either side. Season the inside of the pocket and the entire breast with salt and pepper. Loosely spoon the Swiss chard stuffing into the pocket. Secure the open pocket with skewers or by tying the breast with kitchen twine or heavy string every few inches.

In a large sauté pan, heat the oil to smoking. Add the veal and sear until golden brown on both sides. Transfer the veal to a deep-sided roasting pan and add the stock, raw chopped onion, tomato, and garlic. Cover with aluminum foil.

Place the veal in the oven and cook until done, about 2^1/$_2$ hours, turning the meat once halfway during cooking. If necessary add more stock or water so that the braising liquid covers the veal by two thirds during the entire cooking time.

Transfer the veal to a cutting board and let it rest for 15 minutes before cutting into half-inch-thick slices.

2 tablespoons unsalted butter

1 large onion, finely diced

1 large bunch of Swiss chard, stems trimmed and chopped (about 4 cups)

Sea salt and freshly ground black pepper, to taste

1 2½- to 3-pound breast of veal, boned and trimmed (about 7 pounds bone-in)

1 tablespoon canola oil

4 cups chicken or vegetable stock, or low-sodium canned broth

1 small onion, coarsely chopped

1 tomato, chopped

3 garlic cloves, sliced

Let's Have a Party!

The summer house state of mind makes throwing a party a breeze. There's no need for a whole lot of planning, no discussion of weighty menus or frilly extras to create the right ambience. The casual atmosphere of summer lends itself to a relaxed, buffet-style meal with large bowls of salads and platters of grilled meats and fish. ● These dishes include some of our favorite recipes for entertaining, but when we are planning our parties, we often work around a loose theme that can be carried from the food to the cocktails we serve and even the tablecloth colors we use. So if you're in the mood for a Riviera theme, you can pull together a whole Mediterranean menu from other chapters in the book and double or triple the recipes according to the size of your guest list. And since we are big fans of the all-American spread—and so are the kids— we often pair some of the fancier, make-ahead salads with hot dogs, burgers, and corn from the grill. ● For us, half the fun of planning the party is decorating the buffet table—a large one (or two) if you have it. It's not that important that plates and glasses and napkins match; in fact, we think it's even more fun to mix stuff that doesn't necessarily go together in that artsy, bohemian way (often your only choice in a rental, so it pays to go with it). Flowers from the garden or green market or a big bowl of fruit is all you need to decorate the table.

Then bring on the food—and lots of it. Throw in an ice-cold tub of beer and wine and a pitcher of party drinks. Add your friends and you have a foolproof recipe for a wonderful day.

PARTY TIPS (LEARNED THE HARD WAY)

- Don't sacrifice enjoying your own party with your friends for a fussy menu. The whole point is to have fun and mingle with everyone.
- When you're preparing your dishes, get all of the components for each recipe prepped and ready to go the day before. Then, the next morning, all you have to do is pull the dishes together and do the last-minute grilling.
- Let your friends help. At our houses, the kitchen is where all the energy is, so let people in to give you a hand, even if it's as simple as opening some wine or carrying platters of food outside. (An added plus to having everything prepped is that it makes it easy to have friends toss ingredients together or place salads in bowls).
- A festive cocktail that can be served by the pitcher or a nonalcoholic punch that can be spiked by the glass is always a good ice-breaker during that initial half hour of everyone's arrival.

Chesapeake Crab Dip

MAKES 2 CUPS

Clam dip, good. Crab dip, better! For an extra-extravagant touch, serve raw asparagus spears for dipping.

In a blender or food processor, blend the cream cheese, crème fraîche, lemon juice, and cayenne until smooth. Transfer to a mixing bowl and fold in the crabmeat and chives. Season with salt and pepper.

Cover with plastic wrap and refrigerate until ready to serve.

8 ounces cream cheese

½ cup Crème Fraîche (page 22) or sour cream

Juice of ½ lemon

Pinch of cayenne pepper

8 ounces lump crabmeat, picked over for cartilage

1 tablespoon chopped chives or scallion greens

Sea salt and freshly ground black pepper, to taste

Classic Caesar Dressing

MAKES 1½ CUPS

Okay, we admit it: We love anchovies, and this boldly flavored dressing proves it.

Place the eggs in a pot and cover with water. Bring the water to a boil and allow the eggs to simmer for 2 minutes. Remove the eggs and cool to room temperature. When cool, separate the yolks from the whites, discarding the whites.

In a blender, purée the garlic, mustard, anchovies, and egg yolks until smooth. Add the Worcestershire, lemon juice, vinegar, salt, and pepper and blend again. With the blender on low, drizzle the oil in slowly, blending until the oil emulsifies.

The dressing will keep in the refrigerator for up to 1 week.

3 eggs

3 garlic cloves

1½ tablespoons Dijon mustard

5 anchovy fillets

¼ teaspoon Worcestershire sauce

1 tablespoon lemon juice

1 tablespoon red wine vinegar

¾ teaspoon sea salt

Generous amount of freshly ground black pepper

1 cup extra-virgin olive oil

Grill-Roasted Oysters

SERVES 2 TO 4

One of our favorite memories of visiting the coast of Oregon is a day we spent at Cannon Beach. We opened a crisp bottle of white wine and roasted oysters on the grill. Heating an oyster on the grill until just warm brings out that briny, marine flavor like nothing else. Be careful not to lose even a drop of the oyster liquor when transferring them from the grill; it just might be the best part. Serve the oysters with a simple red wine mignonette sauce that doesn't overpower the delicate ocean flavor of the shellfish.

½ **cup good-quality red wine vinegar**

1 **finely diced shallot**

1 **teaspoon cracked black pepper**

12 **of your favorite oysters**

In a small bowl, stir together the vinegar, shallots, and pepper.

Using tongs, place the oysters on a medium-hot grill. Cook just until they pop open, 10 to 15 minutes, transferring each oyster to a platter as soon as it opens.

To serve, spoon a small amount of the mignonette over each opened oyster.

EAST VERSUS WEST

Choosing the kind of oysters you want from the great variety out there can sometimes seem as challenging as picking the proper bottle of wine to go with them! But there is only one cardinal rule when purchasing oysters: Buy them super-fresh and make sure that you choose ones that have tightly closed shells. After that, it's simply a matter of personal taste and buying whatever is local.

Typically, East Coast oysters are briny and crisp, with a slightly fishy and sometimes pleasantly metallic aftertaste. Our favorites include Malpeque, Pine Island, and Blue Point.

Pacific oysters, on the other hand, are sweeter and sometimes termed fruity. Our two favorites—Kumamoto and Olympia—each have their own distinctive quality. Kumamotos are mild and have a creamy texture, while Olympias taste perfectly clean. Another good choice from the West Coast is Royal Miyagi.

Marinated Bean Salad

SERVES 10

This easy dish takes a bit of time at the stove, making it the perfect recipe for a cloudy afternoon. And when the skies clear, it is a healthy choice to pack up to enjoy at your next picnic. We have used heirloom beans, which come in interesting sizes and colors and are readily available at specialty food shops or health food markets, but limas, navy beans, and flageolets are also good choices. Serve the salad warm so all of the flavors meld together and the vinaigrette just barely clings to the beans.

½ pound dried Calypso beans

½ pound dried Appaloosa beans

½ pound dried Butterscotch beans

1⅓ cups Sherry Shallot Vinaigrette (page 32)

2 teaspoons sea salt

2 tablespoons coarsely chopped fresh thyme leaves

1 tablespoon coarsely chopped fresh rosemary leaves

2 tablespoons coarsely chopped fresh chives

1 tablespoon sherry vinegar (or to taste)

Place each type of bean in its own sauté pan and cover with plenty of water. Bring each pan, uncovered, to a boil over high heat. Reduce the heat to low and cook until tender, about 60 to 70 minutes (larger beans will take longer). See Note.

Drain the beans and place them in a large bowl. While the beans are still warm, add the vinaigrette and salt and toss until the beans are evenly coated. Mix in the herbs and vinegar.

NOTE: Soaking beans overnight will save you cooking time on the stove. If you soak the beans, reduce the simmering time to 40 minutes.

Memorial Day Coleslaw

SERVES 10

There's a bit of kismet to this recipe. Geralyn's coleslaw—a recipe she obtained from her next-door neighbor when she was twelve years old—became her annual contribution to the Memorial Day barbecue dinner her family had each year to kick off the beach season at the Jersey shore. When we compared notes, we were delighted to find that it was amazingly similar to the one Debra grew up with. This is a happy marriage of the two.

In a large bowl, whisk together the mayonnaise, crème fraîche, celery seed, vinegar, and mustard.

Grate the carrots on the medium holes of a vegetable grater.

Add the cabbage and the grated carrots to the dressing and toss until evenly coated. Season with salt and pepper.

Cover with plastic wrap and store in the refrigerator until ready to serve.

1½ cups good-quality prepared mayonnaise or homemade (page 21)

½ cup Crème Fraîche (page 22) or heavy cream

2 teaspoons celery seed

2 tablespoons champagne vinegar

2 tablespoons Dijon mustard

2 carrots

1 medium head Savoy cabbage (1¼ pounds), cored and thinly sliced

1 small head red cabbage (¾ pound), cored and thinly sliced

Sea salt and freshly ground black pepper, to taste

Heirloom Tomato Salad

SERVES 6

We have a serious passion for heirloom tomatoes, and their unique colors and markings make them a beautiful addition to any salad. The "less is more" philosophy certainly holds true for this salad; just combine an interesting variety of tomatoes (zebra, Brandywine, and evergreen are favorites) with some simple seasonings, and toss them all together in a clear glass bowl so that you can see their beautiful colors. Heirloom tomatoes are extra-juicy, so make the salad within an hour of serving so that the juices don't dilute the vinaigrette.

3 pounds assorted ripe heirloom tomatoes

2 tablespoons extra-virgin olive oil

2 tablespoons good-quality balsamic vinegar

2 tablespoons sliced fresh basil (about 6 leaves)

Sea salt and freshly ground black pepper, to taste

Core and cut large tomatoes into 8 wedges; smaller tomatoes can be quartered.

Place the cut tomatoes in a large bowl and drizzle with the oil and vinegar. Add the basil, season with salt and pepper, and gently toss until the tomatoes are evenly coated.

Serve the salad at room temperature.

NOTE: Any leftover salad makes a delectable cold soup the next day when all of the flavors marinate together. To make the soup, simply place any leftover tomatoes, along with the tasty juices left in the bottom of the bowl, in the blender. Process until smooth, taste, and adjust the seasoning with salt, pepper, and a touch of balsamic vinegar if necessary.

Hearty Mediterranean Barley Salad

SERVES 8 TO 10

Every party needs a tried-and-true recipe that you can always rely on. This tasty barley salad is a dream because the barley holds up so well. The addition of cold poached shrimp transforms this from a side dish into an impressive main-course salad.

1 pound white barley, pearl or hulled

1 large zucchini

1 large yellow squash

2 red bell peppers, cored, seeded, and cut into very small, uniform dice

1 tablespoon chopped fresh basil leaves

2 teaspoons chopped fresh thyme leaves

2 tablespoons chopped fresh chives or scallions (white and green parts)

2 tablespoons chopped fresh dill

2 tablespoons chopped fresh flat-leaf parsley

⅔ cup Lemon Vinaigrette (page 31)

Sea salt and freshly ground black pepper, to taste

Place the barley in a large saucepan and cover with water. Bring the water to a boil, reduce the heat, and simmer for 30 to 40 minutes, until the barley is tender. Drain and cool to room temperature.

Trim the ends from the zucchini and squash. Cut the peel along with a generous quarter inch of the flesh from the zucchini and squash. Chop the peel pieces into very small, uniform dice. Reserve the middles of the vegetables for stock or soup.

In a medium bowl, mix together the barley, red pepper, zucchini, and squash. Add the chopped herbs and toss with the vinaigrette. Season with salt and pepper.

Cover with plastic wrap and store in the refrigerator until ready to serve.

Aux Délices Orzo Salad

SERVES 6

This salad is one of Debra's best-sellers at her shop, and so many of her customers have asked for the recipe that she promised to include it in the book. So here it is! Half of its party popularity is due to its compatibility with everything from sandwiches to poached salmon and sliced lamb; the other half lies in its secret ingredient, the ginger oil, which adds an unexpected pungency and sweetness.

⅓ cup unsalted pistachios

Sea salt

8 ounces orzo (a scant 1⅓ cups)

4 ounces dried apricots (about 20), sliced, or 1 cup fresh apricots, (about 4), pitted and diced

1 teaspoon chopped fresh cilantro leaves

¼ teaspoon ground coriander

½ cup scallions (green and white parts), thinly sliced

4 to 5 tablespoons Ginger Oil (page 27)

Freshly ground black pepper, to taste

Juice of ½ lemon

Preheat the oven to 350°F.

Place the nuts on a baking tray and toast in the oven until light golden brown, 6 to 8 minutes.

Bring a medium pot of salted water to a boil over high heat. Add the orzo and cook according to package directions. Drain immediately and rinse with cold water.

In a medium bowl, mix the orzo with the apricots, cilantro, coriander, scallions, and pistachios. Toss with 4 tablespoons of the ginger oil to moisten the pasta. Season with salt and pepper. Drizzle the fresh lemon juice on the salad and toss again. Adjust the seasoning, adding another tablespoon of ginger oil if necessary.

Herb Wrapped Pork Loin with Lemon-Herb Oil

SERVES 8 TO 10

When we were growing up, pork loin was a favorite Sunday afternoon dinner. Debra prefers to serve the pork sliced at room temperature, an added plus for days when everyone is busy and there's no structured dinnertime. Leftover pork makes delicious next-day sandwiches dressed with honey mustard and some spicy arugula greens.

½ cup parsley

¼ cup basil

¼ cup cilantro

1 bunch chives

1 cup extra-virgin olive oil

Zest of 2 lemons

⅛ teaspoon fresh lemon juice

Sea salt and freshly ground black pepper, to taste

½ large bunch of rosemary

½ large bunch of thyme

1 3-pound pork loin

In a blender or food processor, pulse the parsley, basil, cilantro, and chives with a ¹/₂ cup of the oil until the herbs are finely chopped. Add the remaining oil, lemon zest and juice, and salt and pepper, and process until combined. You should have about 1¹/₂ cups of oil.

Place the rosemary and thyme all around the pork loin, securing the herbs with kitchen twine every few inches. Place in a roasting pan, cover with plastic wrap, and refrigerate until ready to cook.

Preheat the oven to 375°F.

Remove the plastic wrap from the pork loin, season with salt and pepper, and cover the meat loosely with aluminum foil. Roast the pork loin for about 25 minutes, or until it is medium-done and a meat thermometer reads 150°F.

Transfer the pork loin to a cutting board and let it rest for 10 to 15 minutes before slicing. Serve warm or at room temperature, generously drizzling the lemon-herb oil over the pork slices.

"Route 27" Pasta Salad

SERVES 10

Route 27, the only road that leads to the Hamptons, happens to be lined with some of the most prolific farm stands we've ever seen on the East Coast. True to the spirit of its name, this pasta salad is made with nearly as many vegetables as penne for a lush confetti of colors and flavor. Be sure to toss in a few more tablespoons of the thyme oil just before serving if you make it ahead of time.

1 pound penne pasta

Sea salt

2 cups fresh peas, or good-quality frozen

24 asparagus spears, woody ends cut off, peeled and cut into 2-inch pieces

Kernels from 2 ears of corn

3 medium carrots, thinly sliced on the bias

25 grape or cherry tomatoes, halved

1 teaspoon fresh thyme leaves

3 tablespoons thinly sliced fresh basil leaves

3 tablespoons fresh flat-leaf parsley, coarsely chopped

Freshly ground black pepper, to taste

1/3 cup Thyme Oil (page 24) or extra-virgin olive oil

Cook the pasta in boiling salted water according to the directions on the package until just al dente. Drain and set aside to cool.

Make an ice-water bath (see tip, page 47).

Steam or boil the peas, asparagus, and corn kernels in separate batches until just tender, about 4 minutes for the peas and asparagus, 5 minutes for the corn. (See Note for microwave instructions.) Drain and transfer to the bowl of ice water until cool. Drain and set aside.

Blanch the carrots in a small pan of boiling water until tender, about 2 minutes. Drain and transfer to the ice-water bath until cool. Drain and set aside.

In an oversized bowl, combine the pasta with the peas, asparagus, corn, carrots, tomatoes, thyme, basil, 1/2 teaspoon salt, and pepper. Add the thyme oil and toss together gently until the pasta is evenly coated. Check for seasoning and adjust if necessary.

NOTE: If you have a microwave, you can prepare the vegetables by placing each in a separate microwave-safe dish. Cover with a lid or plastic wrap and microwave on high as follows: peas, 3 minutes; asparagus, 4 minutes; corn, 2 minutes; carrots, 4 minutes

Asian Sesame Coleslaw

SERVES 6

Almost everyone enjoys this Eastern riff on the traditional coleslaw. The heat of the ginger and jalapeño complements the coolness of the lime juice in a dish that's perfectly suited to a sultry summer day. An added plus: no mayonnaise means no worries about the salad holding up if your buffet table is outdoors.

In a small bowl, mix together the lime juice, soy sauce, sesame and canola oils, jalapeño, and ginger. Set aside.

In a large bowl, mix together the cabbage, carrot, peppers, scallions, cilantro, and sesame seeds. Add the dressing and toss until well mixed. Allow the salad to sit for 5 minutes before serving.

3 tablespoons freshly squeezed lime juice

2 tablespoons soy sauce

1 tablespoon sesame oil

6 tablespoons canola oil

1 tablespoon chopped jalapeño pepper

2 tablespoons peeled and grated fresh ginger (from a 1-inch piece)

5 cups thinly sliced napa cabbage, or 2 cups red cabbage and 3 cups napa

1 large carrot, cut into thin matchsticks

2 medium green bell peppers, cut into thin 2-inch-long strips

½ cup sliced scallions (white and green parts)

¼ cup chopped fresh cilantro leaves

1 tablespoon sesame seeds (optional)

Fiesta Flank Steak

SERVES 6

We dressed up this inexpensive, tasty cut of meat by stuffing it with fresh summer vegetables jelly-roll style. Yet another easy-to-make, impressive-to-serve party dish, the meat can be stuffed a day ahead, cooked the morning of the party, and then served either warm or at room temperature.

2 pounds beef flank steak

8 garlic cloves, thinly sliced

4 shallots, sliced

¾ cup plus 1 tablespoon canola oil

½ zucchini

½ yellow squash

½ eggplant

½ pound spinach, cleaned and stemmed

2 carrots, finely diced

1 teaspoon sea salt

Freshly ground black pepper, to taste

Place the flank steak in a shallow dish. In a small bowl, mix together the garlic, shallots, and $^1/_2$ cup of the oil. Drizzle the oil mixture over the steak, cover with plastic wrap, and place the dish in the refrigerator. Allow the meat to marinate for at least 6 hours, turning the meat over once.

Trim the ends of the zucchini, squash, and eggplant. Cut off the peel along with $^1/_2$ inch of flesh. Cut the peel pieces into $^1/_4$-inch slices and then into small dice.

In a medium sauté pan, heat 1 tablespoon of the oil and sauté the spinach over medium heat until wilted, about 2 minutes. Let cool to room temperature, then chop the spinach roughly, and place in a medium bowl.

In the same sauté pan, add 1 tablespoon of the oil and cook the carrots for 2 to 3 minutes over medium heat, until just tender. Place the carrots in the bowl with the spinach.

Reheat the pan to medium hot with 1 tablespoon of the oil and add the zucchini and squash, cooking until tender, about 3 minutes. Transfer to the bowl of vegetables.

Heat the remaining 2 tablespoons of oil to hot and add the eggplant, cooking until tender, 3 to 4 minutes. Add to the bowl of vegetables. Toss together and season with the salt and pepper.

Preheat the oven to 400°F.

Drain the marinated meat, place it on a cutting board, and lay a sheet of plastic wrap over it. Using a mallet or rolling pin, pound the steak on both sides until it is about $^1/_4$ to $^1/_2$ inch thick throughout. Season with salt and pepper.

Place 2 cups of the vegetables down the center of the meat (use any remaining vegetables in a salad). Roll the meat lengthwise and tie with kitchen string about every 2 inches.

Place the stuffed steak in a baking dish and roast it for 16 to 17 minutes for medium rare. Remove from the oven to a cutting board and allow the meat to rest for 10 to 15 minutes before slicing. Cut the meat in thick slices and arrange on a platter.

Fancy Sweet Corn and Lobster Salad

SERVES 6

An array of bright flavors and bright colors—the sunny yellow of the corn, the rich red of the lobster meat, and the vibrant green of the herbs—puts this salad on the top of our entertainment list. We advise buying cooked and shelled lobster meat at your fishmonger to save you precious prep time, and to prepare all of the other elements a day ahead. All you need to do the day of the party is toss everything together. (Photograph on page 26)

4 cups sweet corn kernels (from 6 to 7 medium ears; see tip, below)

12 ounces cooked lobster meat (about three 1¼-pound lobsters; see page 139)

1 teaspoon chopped fresh thyme leaves

2 teaspoons chopped fresh tarragon leaves

20 grape or cherry tomatoes, halved

⅓ to ½ cup Ginger Vinaigrette (page 33)

Sea salt and freshly ground black pepper, to taste

Place the kernels in a medium saucepan, cover with cold water, and bring to a boil over high heat. Simmer for 2 to 3 minutes, until tender. Drain and rinse under cold water.

Meanwhile, if you are cooking the lobsters yourself, fill an 8-quart pot with salted water and bring to a boil. Plunge the lobsters headfirst into the boiling water, cover, and cook for 11 to 13 minutes.

Carefully remove the lobsters from the pot with tongs. Allow them to cool before removing the meat. Cut the lobster meat from the tails and claws into ³/₄-inch chunks.

In a large bowl, toss the corn kernels with the lobster meat. Add the thyme, tarragon, cherry tomatoes, and ginger vinaigrette. Toss gently until the vinaigrette evenly coats the salad. Season with salt and pepper and add 1 to 2 tablespoons more vinaigrette if needed. Refrigerate, covered, until the salad is chilled.

> **Tip:** One medium-size ear of corn yields about ¾ cup of kernels. To cut the kernels from an ear of corn, break the cob in half. Stand the half on its side and, with a sharp knife, cut starting from the top of the ear and go down, as close to the cob as possible.

Barbecued Tuna

SERVES 8

It took a trip to Texas for us to really embrace the concept of fish tacos, but now we understand all the hoopla— barbecue sauce and fish are truly a scrumptious combo. The earthy seasonings in this ketchup-based sauce work well with any sturdy, meaty fish that is easy to grill, from swordfish and salmon to fresh water trout. The barbecue sauce keeps for a week in the refrigerator.

½ cup ketchup

2 tablespoons soy sauce

1 teaspoon sugar

2 tablespoons red wine vinegar

¼ cup orange juice

2 tablespoons Dijon mustard

2 teaspoons ground cumin

Sea salt and freshly ground pepper, to taste

8 tuna steaks, 1½ inches thick (6 ounces each)

In a medium nonreactive bowl, stir together the ketchup, soy sauce, sugar, vinegar, orange juice, mustard, and cumin. Season with salt and pepper. You will have about 2 cups. Cover with plastic wrap and refrigerate until ready to serve.

To serve, prepare a hot grill.

Season both sides of the tuna steaks with salt and pepper. Transfer 1 cup of the barbecue sauce to a small bowl for basting and brush one side of the steaks with the barbecue sauce.

Place the steaks, sauce side down, on the hot grill and sear them for 1 minute. Baste the other side of the tuna with the sauce, and using tongs, turn the fish over. Let them sear for 1 minute, while basting the tops with another layer of sauce. Turn the steaks again, and let the tuna cook for a minute or two longer. Baste and repeat on the other side of the steaks, grilling the fish until medium rare.

To serve, transfer the tuna steaks to a platter and spoon the remaining barbecue sauce over each.

Simply
Delicious
Desserts

Summer holds some defining memories

about sweets that everyone can relate to: running down the street chasing the neighborhood ice cream truck for your favorite indulgence of the moment or riding your bike to the Dairy Queen for a brain-freezing Slushie or a sugar cone of vanilla and chocolate soft ice cream swirled together. Then there's the Fourth of July tradition of strawberry shortcakes, and the wonderful aroma of fresh fruit pies cooling on the windowsill. ◉ As adults, we still love to indulge in desserts, and while most of us have broadened our culinary horizons from the Dairy Queen days, our cravings still include lots of ice cream. But we also find inspiration at the farm stand when the peaches are perfect or after a morning picking berries with our kids. This chapter both pampers our grown-up palates and includes recipes that appeal to kids—and the kids in us. ◉ Most important, we've tried to keep things really simple, because even the most dedicated bakers need to take some time off to enjoy the great outdoors. Dessert can still be homemade with a few shortcuts: buy disposable muffin tins and cake pans, spend one morning or evening baking a few things and then freeze them to be used in a few days (almost all of these desserts freeze well just for that reason), or serve a homemade item like a fruit soup with store-bought cookies to save time. For those of you who say "Off with the oven" during summer holiday, we suggest fresh fruit compotes and chocolate sauce to drizzle over ice cream, and red wine ice to garnish chilled peach soup.

Chilled White Peach Soup with Red Wine Ice

SERVES 8

Peaches, like tomatoes, should only be eaten in the summer when they are perfectly ripe and bountiful. While we are big fans of peach pie, this simple cold soup showcases the beautiful white peaches that are so abundant in August. Don't overlook this dessert soup's possibility as a refreshing first course for a summer supper, especially nice if you are eating outdoors.

8 ripe white peaches, peeled, pitted, and cut into chunks

¾ cup Riesling

1¼ cups Simple Syrup (page 36)

1¼ cups freshly squeezed orange juice (from 4 medium oranges)

2 cups freshly squeezed lemon juice (from 2 large lemons)

1½ cups Red Wine Ice (opposite)

Mint sprigs, for garnish

Place the peach chunks in a blender with the wine, simple syrup, orange juice, and lemon juice and purée until smooth. Strain the liquid through a fine strainer and chill, covered, in the refrigerator until ready to serve.

To serve, ladle a cup of the soup into a bowl and garnish with 2 to 3 tablespoons of red wine ice and a sprig of mint.

Red Wine Ice

MAKES 8 TO 10 GARNISH SERVINGS OR 4 DESSERT PORTIONS

Perhaps the best use for a leftover bottle of red wine that we could ever think of, this icy concoction is surprisingly simple to make and doesn't require any equipment other than your freezer. We like to pair this with desserts like the Chilled White Peach Soup, but it also makes a nice palate cleanser just before the dessert course, or can be served as dessert on its own with biscotti or your favorite cookies.

2 cups sugar

¼ cup water

¾ teaspoon grated lemon zest

¾ teaspoon grated orange zest

½-750 ml bottle red Burgundy wine, or other good-quality red wine

½ cup orange juice

½ cup peach nectar

In a large saucepan, bring all of the ingredients to a boil over high heat, stirring occasionally. When the liquid boils, remove from the heat and let it cool to room temperature.

Pour the red wine mixture into an 8 × 8-inch rectangular stainless-steel baking pan. Place in the freezer, stirring every 20 to 30 minutes with a whisk. Continue this procedure until the mixture is slushy, 2 to 3 hours. Before serving, run a fork through the ice for granules.

Fourth of July Shortcakes

SERVES 8

This is one dessert that carries us right back to childhood berry-picking adventures and Fourth of July picnic celebrations. While store-bought shortcakes are always okay in a pinch, these only take about 10 minutes to put together, so we have a hard time convincing ourselves not to make them fresh.

1 pint raspberries

1 pint blueberries

1 pint strawberries, hulled and cut into quarters

¼ cup orange juice

⅓ cup plus 1 teaspoon granulated sugar

3 cups all-purpose flour

½ teaspoon cinnamon

2½ teaspoons baking soda

¾ cup (1½ sticks) chilled butter, cut into cubes

1½ tablespoons grated orange zest

¾ cup buttermilk

2 cups plus 2 tablespoons heavy cream

3 tablespoons confectioners' sugar

In a medium bowl, mix together the berries and orange juice. Cover with plastic and refrigerate for at least an hour to allow the fruit to release its juices.

Preheat the oven to 350°F.

In a mixer with the paddle attachment or by hand in a medium bowl, combine ⅓ cup of the granulated sugar, the flour, cinnamon, and baking soda. Add the cubed butter and mix on a slow speed or by hand using a pastry cutter until the batter has a cornmeal consistency. Be careful not to overmix. The batter should not come together at this point.

Mix in the orange zest, then the buttermilk by hand. Combine until the batter is moist, but not sticky.

Remove the dough from the bowl and roll it out until it is ¼ to ½ inch thick. Cut into eight 3-inch rounds (an empty, cleaned can makes a good biscuit cutter). Brush the tops with 2 tablespoons of the heavy cream and sprinkle with the remaining teaspoon of granulated sugar.

Bake for 25 minutes, rotating the pan 180 degrees after 10 minutes, until the shortcakes are golden brown.

Meanwhile, in a medium bowl, whip the remaining 2 cups of heavy cream and the confectioners' sugar together until stiff peaks form. Refrigerate, covered, until ready to serve.

To serve, split the shortcakes in half and place the bottom halves on a serving platter. Spoon the berry mixture over the shortcakes and top with the whipped cream. Cover with the remaining shortcake halves.

Strawberry Basil Compote

MAKES 1¼ CUPS

During her last trip to Provence, Debra found a wonderful small shop in Saint-Rémy owned by critically acclaimed chocolate artisan Joël Durand. She spent a wonderful afternoon sampling many of his chocolates, but it was the strawberry basil jam that made the truly lasting impression. This is her version. Spoon it over ice cream or pound cake for dessert, or enjoy it anytime slathered on buttered toast.

½ cup orange juice

4 generous cups medium to large strawberries (about 30), stems removed and cut in half

20 large fresh basil leaves, chopped

1 teaspoon grated lemon zest

1 tablespoon honey

1 tablespoon balsamic vinegar

2 fresh mint leaves, chopped

In a medium nonreactive saucepan, bring the orange juice, strawberries, basil, lemon zest, and honey to a boil over medium heat. Reduce heat to low and simmer until the juice is thick and syrupy, about 10 minutes. Stir in the vinegar, remove from the heat, and cool to room temperature. Stir in the chopped mint, and serve.

Decadently Dark Chocolate Sauce

MAKES 2⅓ CUPS

Do you remember riding your bike after dinner in the dusk to Dairy Queen for one of their to-die-for hot fudge sundaes? We sure do, and this easy chocolate sauce, drizzled over ice cream or fresh strawberries, is our adult version of a childhood vice we've never quite grown out of.

2 cups heavy cream

5 ounces best-quality bittersweet chocolate, cut into pieces

2 tablespoons unsalted butter

In a heavy, non-aluminum saucepan, bring the cream to a boil. Place the chocolate in a medium bowl and pour the hot cream over it. Let the cream soften the chocolate for about 2 minutes. Whisk the cream and chocolate together, then add the butter and whisk until completely smooth.

Transfer to a glass or plastic container and cover tightly. The sauce will keep in the refrigerator for up to 2 weeks. To reheat, microwave on low or melt in a saucepan over low heat, stirring occasionally.

Bittersweet Beachside Brownies

MAKES 12 BROWNIES

While these dark chocolate squares have a decidedly adult edge, we find that the kids love them as much as we do. For a special treat, the brownies can be transformed into homemade ice cream sandwiches or sundaes, topped with Decadently Dark Chocolate Sauce (page 173). To make ice cream sandwiches, just cut the brownies in half horizontally and sandwich a half-inch-thick slab of your favorite ice cream flavor—vanilla, chocolate, coffee, strawberry, or pistachio are our picks—between the slices.

Preheat the oven to 350°F.

In a medium saucepan over medium-low heat, melt the chocolate with the butter, stirring occasionally. Set aside.

In a large bowl, whisk together the eggs and both sugars. Stir in the melted chocolate and butter. Stir in the vanilla.

In a separate bowl, combine the flour, baking soda, and cinnamon. Stir the flour mixture into the chocolate mixture until well combined.

Grease a 13 × 9-inch pan with nonstick cooking spray or the tablespoon of butter. Pour the batter into the pan and bake for 30 to 40 minutes, until a toothpick comes out clean. Let the brownies cool to room temperature before cutting into 3-inch squares.

1½ **pounds good-quality bittersweet chocolate, chopped**

1 **cup plus 2 tablespoons (2¼ sticks) unsalted butter**

6 **large eggs**

¾ **cup granulated sugar**

1 **cup plus 2 tablespoons (packed) dark brown sugar**

1½ **teaspoons vanilla extract**

1½ **cups all-purpose flour**

¼ **teaspoon baking soda**

½ **teaspoon cinnamon**

Nonstick cooking spray or 1 tablespoon unsalted butter, to grease the pan

Creamy Citrus Mousse

SERVES 6

Who doesn't love that creamy, cloudlike texture of a classic mousse? While the traditional chocolate is way too heavy for a summer menu, this citrus mousse hits just the right note. The pink grapefruit juice adds a cool, refreshing flavor with a hint of sweetness.
(Photograph on page 166)

- 1½ tablespoons powdered unflavored gelatin
- ¾ cup ruby red grapefruit juice
- ½ cup plus 1 tablespoon freshly squeezed lemon juice (from 2 to 3 large lemons)
- 1 cup sugar
- 8 eggs
- 6 tablespoons (¾ stick) unsalted butter, cut into pieces
- 2 cups Crème Fraîche (page 22)

Place 4 tablespoons water in a small bowl. Sprinkle the gelatin over the water and let it stand until the gelatin is soft, about 10 minutes.

In a double boiler, whisk the grapefruit and lemon juices, sugar, eggs, and butter together. Stir over simmering water until the butter melts and mixture thickens, 8 to 10 minutes. Add the softened gelatin mixture and stir until it dissolves. Remove from the heat and let cool to room temperature.

Meanwhile, beat the crème fraîche in a medium bowl with an electric mixer or whisk until soft peaks form. Gently fold into the cooled citrus mixture. Divide the mousse into 6 pretty cups or pour into a 6-cup mold and chill until firm.

> **Tip:** If you don't have a double boiler, set a medium stainless-steel bowl over a medium saucepan—just make sure the bottom of the bowl doesn't touch the simmering water.

Fig and Honey Compote

MAKES 1¾ CUPS

Whether it's the green Calimyrna figs of spring and early summer or the Black Mission variety that late summer brings, fresh figs are simply one of our favorite fruits. They are positively ambrosial transformed into this rich compote and served over vanilla ice cream. In the winter, dried figs or dates make good substitutes for the fresh, served with warm pound cake or angel food cake.

12 fresh ripe figs, quartered

3 tablespoons honey

¾ cup orange juice

¾ teaspoon grated lemon zest

3 teaspoons balsamic vinegar

In a small saucepan, combine the figs, honey, orange juice, and lemon zest. Cook over medium heat for 8 to 10 minutes, until syrupy. Stir in the vinegar and simmer for 2 more minutes. Cool to room temperature and serve with vanilla ice cream, pound cake, or angel food cake.

Fig and Raspberry Fool

SERVES 4 TO 5

While this old-fashioned English dessert is traditionally made with berries, we've updated it by adding fresh figs (we'll find any excuse to use them). If you aren't as obsessed with figs as we are, large strawberries make an excellent stand-in. And for cooler climes, try a good ruby port instead of the Riesling for a rich, nutty flavor.

1 cup heavy cream

1 tablespoon confectioners' sugar (optional)

1 cup Riesling Beaumes-de-Venise, or other sweet white wine

1 tablespoon granulated sugar

14 figs, preferably Black Mission, ends cut off, quartered

½ pint raspberries

1 cup Crème Fraîche (page 22)

Raw sugar, for garnish (optional)

With a mixer or by hand, whip the cream and confectioners' sugar together until the mixture forms soft peaks. Set aside.

In a medium sauté pan over medium-high heat, bring the wine, granulated sugar, and figs to a boil. Reduce the heat to low and allow the fruit to simmer until the juice becomes thick and syrupy. Stir in the raspberries and cook until they are soft, 3 to 4 minutes. Remove the pan from the heat and let cool to room temperature.

Strain the juice from the fruit mixture and reserve.

Meanwhile, whisk the crème fraîche into the whipped cream. Stir in the reserved juice.

To serve, spoon a generous 2 tablespoons of the whipped-cream mixture into clear parfait glasses. Spoon 2 tablespoons of cooked fruit on the cream. Repeat the process to form a second layer. Garnish with a sprinkle of raw sugar, if you wish.

Luscious Lemon Cake

SERVES 6 TO 8

This light-as-air cake is the perfect vacation dessert because it can be whipped up in less than 15 minutes. It is so moist that it doesn't need a frosting, though it looks pretty sprinkled with powdered sugar. Top a slice with a dollop of the Strawberry Basil Compote (page 172) for another nice way to dress things up at dinner or for a special treat the next day for breakfast.

¾ cup (1½ sticks) plus 1 tablespoon unsalted butter, softened

1 cup sugar

2 large eggs

1 tablespoon grated lemon zest

1 teaspoon vanilla or lemon extract

1 cup all-purpose flour

½ teaspoon baking powder

½ teaspoon baking soda

⅛ teaspoon salt

⅓ cup sour cream

Preheat the oven to 350°F.

In a medium bowl, cream together the butter with the sugar, scraping the sides of the bowl. Add the eggs one at a time, mixing well. Stir in the lemon zest and vanilla extract.

In a separate bowl, mix together the flour, baking powder, baking soda, and salt. Add the dry ingredients to the wet ingredients, stirring until well incorporated. Stir in the sour cream and blend well.

Grease a round 9-inch baking pan with the remaining tablespoon of butter. Spoon the batter into the pan and place it on a rack in the middle of the oven. Bake the cake for 30 to 40 minutes, until a toothpick inserted in the middle of the cake comes out clean.

Stormy-Day Banana Bread

MAKES TWO 9 × 5-INCH LOAVES

Back in the days before video games and movies on DVD, a stormy day called for creative kid management. This was one of our favorite things to mix together with our moms, who cleverly kept all of the ingredients on hand. Whether it's toasted and bathed in butter for breakfast or topped with jam or our Fig and Honey Compote (page 177) for an afternoon snack, an entire loaf will surely be gone in a snap—that's why we always make a second as backup.

1¼ cups (2½ sticks) unsalted butter

3⅛ cups sugar

5 eggs

1¾ teaspoons vanilla extract

6 very ripe bananas, cut into medium chunks

6 cups all-purpose flour

2½ teaspoons baking soda

2½ teaspoons baking powder

¾ teaspoon sea salt

1¼ cups sour cream

1½ cups walnuts (optional)

Nonstick cooking spray or 1 tablespoon plus 1 teaspoon unsalted butter, to grease the pans

Preheat the oven to 350°F. Coat two 9 × 5-inch loaf pans with nonstick spray or butter.

Using a mixer with a paddle attachment, or in a large bowl by hand, cream the butter and sugar together, occasionally scraping the sides of the bowl. Add the eggs one at a time. Stir in the vanilla.

Stir in the bananas, piece by piece; if you are mixing by hand, mash the banana pieces before stirring them in.

In a separate bowl, combine the flour, baking soda, baking powder, and salt. Stir a portion of the dry ingredients into the wet ingredients, alternating with some of the sour cream. Repeat until the ingredients are well combined. If you are using the walnuts, stir them in.

Divide the batter between the loaf pans. Bake in the oven for an hour or until a toothpick comes out clean.

Perfect Peach Pie

SERVES 6 TO 8

Every summer Debra takes her children to Wightman's farm to pick peaches, just the same way her mom used to take Deb and her sister when they were little. And then they go home and bake. Since this pie is all about the peaches, patiently waiting until the local ones are perfectly ripe is well worth it. A scoop of vanilla ice cream on top may be gilding the lily, but hey, live a little!

2 portions One and Only Pie Crust (page 185)

7 to 8 ripe peaches

⅜ cup all-purpose flour

¾ cup plus 1 teaspoon sugar

1¼ teaspoons cinnamon

1 teaspoon freshly squeezed lemon juice

3 tablespoons unsalted butter, melted

2 tablespoons heavy cream

Preheat the oven to 350°F.

Roll out one pie crust and fit it into a 9-inch pie tin, leaving a 1-inch overhang. Refrigerate the crust for 15 minutes.

Cut the peaches into 8 pieces each, discarding the pits. In a large bowl, toss the peaches with the flour, ³/₄ cup of the sugar, the cinnamon, lemon juice, and butter. Toss until the peaches release their juices and all of the flour and sugar have dissolved.

Place the peach mixture into the chilled pie shell. Roll out the second pie crust into a 9-inch circle and fit it over the peach mixture. Bring up the overhanging crust to seal the top and flute the edges. Cut some decorative vents in the top.

Mix together the heavy cream and the remaining teaspoon of sugar until the sugar dissolves. Brush the mixture on the top and the edges of the crust.

Place the pie on a baking sheet on the center rack of the oven. Bake for 40 to 45 minutes, until the peaches are bubbling and the crust is golden brown. Check the pie as it bakes; if the crust starts to get too dark, cover it with aluminum foil.

Raspberry Pie

SERVES 6 TO 8

Ten pints of raspberries? You bet. This beautiful pie deserves an entire morning dedicated to berry picking because it's the intensely sweet, ripe berries that make it top our list of favorite summer treats. That great texture in each bite comes from mixing lots of whole berries into the puréed berries. It's too good for a garnish, so we serve this straight up.

1 portion One and Only Pie Crust (opposite)

10 pints fresh raspberries

1¼ cups sugar

5 tablespoons cornstarch

2 tablespoons freshly squeezed lemon juice

Preheat the oven to 450°F.

Roll out the pie crust and fit it into a 9-inch pie tin, leaving a 1-inch overhang. Trim and flute the edge. Prick the bottom of the crust with a fork.

Place the pie crust in the middle rack of the oven and bake until golden brown, about 15 minutes.

Meanwhile, in a blender purée 6¹/₂ pints of the raspberries until smooth.

In a medium, nonreactive saucepan, mix together the sugar and cornstarch. Whisk in the lemon juice. Strain the raspberry purée through a fine sieve into the pan.

Bring the raspberry mixture to a boil over medium heat, stirring constantly. Let the mixture boil for a minute, until it thickens. Remove from the heat and gently stir in the remaining raspberries until they are thoroughly mixed into the purée.

Pour the raspberry mixture into the pie shell and refrigerate for at least 4 hours or overnight.

The One and Only Pie Crust Recipe You'll Ever Need

MAKES FOUR 9-INCH PIE CRUSTS

Perfectly light and flaky every time, this pie crust works well with all kinds of fillings. Even if you are baking only one pie, make the entire recipe anyway, as the dough freezes beautifully.

4 cups all-purpose flour

2 teaspoons sugar

1 teaspoon sea salt

1¾ cups plus 2 tablespoons solid vegetable shortening

1 large egg

2 tablespoons champagne vinegar

1 tablespoon water

Place the flour, sugar, and salt in a large bowl. Add the shortening and mix with a fork until crumbly.

In a separate bowl, mix together the egg, vinegar, and water. Add the egg mixture to the flour mixture and combine until the flour is moistened. Divide into 4 portions, shaping each into a disc. Wrap each disc in plastic and refrigerate at least 30 minutes before rolling out.

NOTE: The pie crusts can be refrigerated up to 1 week or frozen up to 1 month; defrost the crust overnight in the refrigerator before rolling.

acknowledgments

To our agent, Jane Dystel, who enthusiastically did what she does best—she made this book happen!

To our creative editor, Pam Krauss, whose vision for this book kept us focused and on track. To the wonderful Adina Steiman for her suggestions and editing skills.

To the talented Maggie Hinders for her delightfully fresh and fun book design. To Mark McCauslin for his fabulous vintage linens.

To Mark Ferri for his beautiful photography, his willingness to work long days to catch the best sunlight on both ends of the day, and his easygoing, fun-to-work-with nature.

To Debra's staff at Aux Délices, who kept things running so smoothly during those long hours of recipe testing and editing; a special thanks to everyone in the kitchen, who always came to our rescue when we needed second rounds of ingredients to test and who did an amazing job of organizing all of the food for the 5 A.M. photo shoots!

To Geralyn's staff at her public relations agency, Resources, especially Andrea Abrams and Anita Fresolone, for keeping it all together at the office when deadlines were pressing.

To Geralyn's friends in Saratoga Springs, New York, especially Seth Berger, who gave her a quiet place to escape for some focused writing time, and David Meyers, whose support and enthusiasm provided her with an ongoing excitement to write every weekend.

index